Your Thoughts Matter

The Future You Are Creating Starts Now

Reflections and Affirmations

ANTOINETTE PELLEGRINI

Copyright © Antoinette Pellegrini 2017

Published by Busybird Publishing

ISBN 9781925585537

Photography by Antoinette Pellegrini

Photo Editing by Andrew Szczurko

This book is copyright. Apart from any fair dealing for the purposes of study, research, criticism, review, or as otherwise permitted under the Copyright Act, no part may be reproduced by any process without written permission. Enquiries should be made through the publisher.

Dedication

For everyone who has a dream but feels they cannot ever achieve it – my message to you is that anything is possible. Change your thinking, believe it is possible, take action one step at a time and you can make it happen.

For my sons, Andrew and Robert – this book is my gift to you. It captures my thoughts, beliefs and my aspirations. It is my advice to you, to remind you of who you are and how powerful you can be when you direct your life through conscious choices. Thank you for helping me to finish this book.

For my family and friends and all the people who have touched my life and made a difference to me, thank you for being there for me.

For my father Rocco, who passed over in April 2005. I promised him I would complete this book.

Contents

Preface	i
An Overview: Your Thoughts Matter	v
Reflections and Affirmations	1
Affirmation 1	3
1 Your Future is Created Now	5
Affirmation 2	9
2 Origins	11
Affirmation 3	15
3 The Source of Your Creative Power	17
Affirmation 4	21
4 Who Are You?	23
Affirmation 5	27
5 You Are a Creator	29
Affirmation 6	33
6 Trust Your Intuition	35
Affirmation 7	39
7 Imagination	41
Affirmation 8	45
8 Freedom to Choose	47
Affirmation 9	51
9 Your Attitude Matters	53
Affirmation 10	57
10 Conscious Choice	59
Affirmation 11	63
11 Dare to Be Yourself	65

Affirmation 12	69
12 Embrace Your Feelings	71
Affirmation 13	75
13 Understand Your Fears	77
Affirmation 14	81
14 Recognise the Ties That Bind	83
Affirmation 15	87
15 Being	89
Affirmation 16	93
16 Gratitude	95
Affirmation 17	99
17 Choose Happiness	101
Affirmation 18	105
18 Purpose	107
Affirmation 19	111
19 Mirrors	113
Affirmation 20	117
20 Show the Way	119
Affirmation 21	121
21 Love	123
Affirmation 22	127
22 You Have the Power	129
Affirmation 23	133
23 You Make a Difference	135
Affirmation 24	139
24 Our World	141
Affirmation 25	145
25 Infinity	147
About The Author	151

Preface

This book is for anyone who is starting to question who they are and where they fit in the world. It is for those who are searching for something beyond themselves, those who may feel disempowered or unable to achieve their dreams or for those who just feel that there must be more to life.

My message is that you are more powerful than you realise and that power is within you. You make a difference and your influence is much greater than you imagine, and it all starts with your thinking.

Thoughts are the basis of what you are creating in your life. Nothing can be done or achieved unless you think of it first. More than this, thought is an energy vibration, attracting similar vibrations. What you are thinking now is creating what and who you will be tomorrow.

Your thoughts can be your best friend or your worst enemy. Every thought is an affirmation – either positive or negative. What is your self-talk saying to you about yourself? If your thoughts are not positive, you can change that. It is your choice. Rather than focusing on the negative, or on what you don't have, you can make a decision that you deserve to be happy, that you are worthy, that you will view life positively and with gratitude for everything you do have.

You are in control of what you think. No one can take this away from you. It is my hope that this book may in some way assist you to feel empowered to be the person you want to be and achieve what you want from life.

This book is also about recognising the connection between all of creation and your connection to everything in existence – All That Is.[1] The separation that we feel from each other is not real. Our lives are a journey towards oneness, towards discovering the connection we all have. It is a journey to being whole.

The Reflections in the book are designed to empower and inspire you to contemplate, discuss and even meditate on the ideas and concepts. Each Reflection starts with a quote. Many of the quotes will be known to you. I chose them as a way of introducing the concepts in each Reflection.

Each Reflection has an accompanying Affirmation which captures the essence of the Reflection. The photographs with each Affirmation were taken by me and are intended to evoke the feelings, emotions and themes of the Reflection.

The messages repeat throughout this book deliberately. They are not new messages. Many spiritual and self development books carry the same messages of personal empowerment. How the messages are put together in this book is my own.

The messages build as the book progresses so I recommend that you read the book from beginning to end at least once. After that, you may just wish to go to a particular Reflection or Affirmation that you want to re-read or you may wish to use the book as an oracle, opening it to a particular page for a message relevant to you at the time.

---

[1] Neale Donald Walsch, *Conversations with God: An Uncommon Dialogue Book 1*, Hodder Headline Australia, 1995

The term "All That Is" comes from this book. I have used the term "All That Is" to refer to the Universal Energy, the "Whole", what some may call "God" or the "Source". Pages 22 to 26 in *Conversations with God* have a fuller description of the concept of "God" as "All That Is".

It is my hope you will pick up this book again and again – to meditate, feel empowered or to reflect on any messages that are significant or needed at that time. In this way, you will experience something different and take from the book what you need at the time.

The Reflections start with a free form poem, *Your Future is Created Now*. It sums up the message in the book that we have the power to create our own reality through our thoughts, emotions and our choices. The Reflections end with another free form poem, *Infinity*, for there really is no end; there is only the journey.

I hope you enjoy this experience.

An Overview

Your Thoughts Matter

We are not bystanders in this world. We are creators. We cannot stand back thinking that we have no influence on what happens in the world. We are participants and creators of our own reality through our thoughts, feelings and choices, whether we realise it or not.

Imagine how you would feel if you were able to create the life you want? How would you feel if you were happy and fulfilled, knowing that you were in control and able to handle any situation that came your way. You can achieve this and it all starts with your thoughts.

Our thinking is influenced by our identity – how we see ourselves, and this in turn creates our values, beliefs and attitude. Our beliefs and attitude become reflected in our behaviour and ultimately the outcomes we have in our lives.

The issue is that how we see ourselves can often be influenced by the messages and values of others. We receive messages every day from family, friends, colleagues, the media, and now in particular, social media. Do you see yourself as someone who is strong, confident and able to achieve what you want? Or have you been influenced by messages you have received from others, implying that you will never be good enough, smart enough or attractive enough?

Thoughts repeated become embedded – creating neural links in your brain, reinforcing patterns of thinking and behaviour – positive and negative. More than this, thought is an energy vibration, as is everything else in the universe. Your thoughts are energy that attracts similar energy. Your thinking connects you to everything else. There is a universal bond that connects us all. Science, through the study of quantum physics, is starting to discover that bond – the connection that we literally have with everything in our universe, and possibly beyond.

The future exists as possibilities and all possibilities are open to you. We exist in an interconnected universe of energy that links us to everyone and everything. The future exists as a wave of possibilities. We change those possibilities into reality by our thoughts, feelings, actions and choices.

You are the creator of your life and your future. Even when things happen unexpectedly or that seem to be outside your control, you always have control over how you respond to what happens.

Do you know what you want in life? More time, more friends? More money so that you can leave a job you don't like, go on a holiday or just have more time to do the things you want to do? Do you buy a lottery ticket every week, hoping that a big win will enable you to achieve the things you want? We all know enough stories about people who won the lottery and who after a few years are unhappier and have less money than ever before.

Ultimately, what most people want is to be happy. Happiness is one of the key drivers of what we do. Almost every action we take is to achieve happiness now or in the future. We even put up with and endure things we don't like – an unfulfilling job or a bad relationship, to achieve future happiness – enough to eat, a nice place to live, money for a holiday, or to avoid an alternative that we fear would bring more unhappiness.

If happiness is one of our key drivers, then why are so many people unhappy? Happiness is not found "out there". To empower yourself to create the happiness you seek you first need to regain control of your thinking, regain your power. This is not external, happiness is not external, it is a way of being, a way of thinking. To change your life and to regain control of how you feel – you need to change the way you think.

That's the good news. It is up to you, it is within your control, no matter what your circumstances are. You can control how you feel and respond to what is happening. You can create new neural links in your brain, more positive ones that will bring you joy and happiness. You are in control of your thoughts and how you feel – no one can take this away from you, and how you feel is the key to empowering yourself to create the life you want.

Our whole world, our reality - everyone and everything around us – is a mirror reflecting our mind, our emotions and our thoughts. You can create the life you dream of. Be conscious of what you are dreaming of and create the life you would like to live.

One of the best ways to begin to change your thinking is to adopt an attitude of gratitude. Being thankful for the things you have begins to change negative thinking into positive thought patterns.

We often go through the day without appreciating or thinking about all the good things in our lives, focusing instead on what we don't have or what is missing in our lives. Gratitude and appreciation means focusing on what we do have.

No matter who you are and what situation you find yourself in, there is always something to be grateful for. The one thing we all have is the amazing gift of life and with life comes opportunity and possibility for change. We have sunlight, nature, air to breathe and water to drink. Think about all the positives in your life and the many things that support our life that we often take for granted.

Appreciation and gratitude is a positive, uplifting feeling which creates happiness and connects us to the present moment. Regularly practising and feeling gratitude creates new neural pathways in the brain, leading to more positive patterns, thoughts, feelings and behaviours.

Not only will positive thoughts start attracting like energies and positivity into your life, you can literally start to change your body chemistry and improve your overall health and well being. Your thoughts and feelings, positive or negative, literally change your physiology. You are a connected whole - mind, body and spirit. What affects one part affects all parts.

With thought comes another great gift – imagination. Your imagination allows you to be and do anything you want. Dream and create a positive vision for yourself. Your brain and your body chemistry reacts in the same way, positively or negatively, to something you vividly imagine as it does to an actual experience.

There are other ways to change our pattern of thinking. Positive affirmations can work, as thoughts repeated create the neural linkages in the brain. Meditation, creativity and simply having fun, doing things that you enjoy, will create positivity and improve health and well-being, which in turn, creates more positivity and happiness.

Your thoughts, feelings and actions are all energy vibrations acting as magnets to similar vibrations, both internally within your mind, body and spirit, and externally, creating the circumstances that make up your life. This is happening whether you are aware of it or not. Being aware of the future you are creating for yourself and for others, you become empowered to become an active creator – consciously directing the course of your life.

Your thoughts matter.

Reflections and Affirmations

Affirmation 1

I Create My Future Now

I create the future

Turning possibilities into reality

Through my thoughts, feelings, actions and choices

I create my future NOW

I create it consciously

I make a difference

No one will ever be like me

My existence changes the world

1

Your Future is Created Now

It is not in the stars to hold our
Destiny but in ourselves.
William Shakespeare (1564 – 1616)

You are creating your future right now, in this moment, while you are reading these words.

The first and last Reflections in this book are free-form poems. The message in this one is that you create your own reality through your thoughts, emotions and choices, attracting like energies and changing future possibilities into your reality.

All possibilities are open to you. It is your choice to create your future unconsciously, seemingly at the whim of fate or destiny, or consciously, with a clear vision and objectives, knowing that you are the creator of your life. Empower yourself to be a more powerful creator of the life you want to have.

You create the future

Turning possibilities into reality

Through your thoughts and your choices

You create it now, for you and everyone

You are important. You matter

The world is not the same without you

Embrace your experiences

Wonderful experiences and sad ones too

All your experiences have meaning

Your experiences are what make you

Yet the truth is, you make your experiences

You are the creator

Have no fear

Know that you are never alone

Listen to your intuition

To your heart – the voice inside you

It is the key to your soul

To who you really are

All your decisions are yours

You have free will to choose

You choose your thoughts, feelings and responses

No-one can take this freedom away

And through these choices you create

You create your future today

You are part of a universal energy

Never ending, always changing

An eternal renewal

You are a reflection of the world

The world is a reflection of you

Yet you are unique

You make a difference

No one will ever be like you

Your very existence changes the world

You create the future

You create it NOW

Create it consciously

Affirmation 2

My Origins

I am one with the energy of creation

Created from one source

I am connected to everything in the universe

Every part affects the whole

I am an intrinsic part of that whole

It is not complete without me

I matter

2

Origins

Humankind has not woven the web of life.
We are but one thread within it.
Whatever we do to the web, we do to ourselves.
All things are bound together.
All things connect.
Chief Seattle (c1760 – 1866)

Imagine everything that exists, all that is, as an enormous stretch of sand, beautiful golden sand stretching as far as you can see in all directions. Now imagine that this is all there is in existence.

Out of that sand spring sandcastles – all different shapes and sizes, some huge and magnificent, others little more than bumps in the sand. The distances between them are all different too. Some very close and some far apart – so far apart that they seem like tiny specks. They all spring up at different times. Some are very old and some only very recently created. From the vantage point of each sandcastle, they are separate, distinct objects.

Imagine that you are one of the sandcastles – you can make yourself into anything you want – it's up to you. You see the other sandcastles – they are all so different. Some are similar to you – others so strange they bear no resemblance. You see yourself as an individual – you are separate from them.

But in reality, each sandcastle is made of the same thing, each is connected, each is a part of the sand from which they were created. They are one. No matter when each separate sandcastle was created, both new and old existed always – only their shape changes. When a sandcastle collapses it merges back into the sand from where it came, to be reborn as something else – never dying. It can't die because it is part of the whole – part of the All That Is.

Like the sandcastle, you are both individual and one with everything else in existence.

Think about everything that exists in our universe. It all appears as vastly different – animate and inanimate, conscious and unconscious, seemingly lifeless objects, man-made and natural – but appearances are deceiving. At their core, the energy and particles that make up all things in our universe are the same - like different "sandcastles" made from the same "sand".

We are children of the stars.

Science tells us that the universe was created from the "Big Bang", an instant in time from which everything we know was created. We originate from the energy that exploded at creation. Before that moment our universe did not exist. Everything in our universe was formed from the energy released at that moment.

All existence, animate and inanimate, is the product of the same ninety-two elements that came from the energy of creation. These are the elements that make up everything in the universe - the stars and the planets and us. They are the same elements that form our DNA and the DNA of every creature on Earth.

Cells are patterns of molecules. Molecules are patterns of atoms and atoms are patterns of subatomic particles. Subatomic particles are energy – they are not "made up" of energy – they are energy.[2] They are the energy that makes up everything we know of in existence.

We are energy and everything that exists is energy.

Einstein confirmed this with his famous equation, $E=MC^2$,[3] which tells us that matter, energy and mass are equivalent - they are the same thing. Matter is energy condensed and vibrating at different levels and intensities.

Even the most seemingly lifeless things, such as rocks, or the inanimate objects we make, such as tables and chairs, are energy. They have atoms vibrating within them. Even plants respond to stimuli with what appear to be reactions similar to ours. Time-lapse photography has shown that plants retract from pain, respond to music and to positive words.[4] The difference is that their reactions are much slower than ours. Many seemingly inanimate things such as rocks and even man-made structures could possibly display the same reactions, if only we had the means to be able to capture them.

Certainly, the implications of quantum physics blur the distinction between organic and inorganic. Subatomic particles – the building blocks of matter, are not lifeless. Experiments have shown that subatomic particles, which are the energy

---

2 Gary Zukav, *The Dancing Wu Li Masters: An Overview of the New Physics*, Rider & Co, UK, 1979. This edition published 1991, Rider & Co, page 212

This book is an explanation and exploration of developments in quantum mechanics without the mathematics. It also links these developments with eastern mysticism.

3 Albert Einstein, *Relativity: The Special and General Theory; A Popular Exposition*, translated by Robert W Lawson, Crown Publishers, New York, 1961, page 48

This is a book by Albert Einstein in which he explains his theory of General and Special Relativity in simple to understand language.

4 Gary Zukav, *The Dancing Wu Li Masters: An Overview of the New Physics*, page 71

of which everything is made up, appear to make decisions and these decisions seem to be based on and instantaneously affected by, decisions made elsewhere, often many miles away.[5]

Science is also telling us that there is an invisible force connecting all of this energy together.

Therefore, the energy that makes up matter is 'alive' and it is connected to energy everywhere. The only difference between all of the different things that make up the universe is how the energy is combined.

The physical law of mass-energy, is that the total amount of mass-energy in the universe is, and always will be, the same. Energy may change to mass and mass may change to energy, but the total energy of the universe remains the same.[6]

The energy that came into existence at creation never dies; it just changes form. Like the changing shapes of the sandcastles on the beach, it is formed and reformed again and again.

You are that energy. We all are that energy. Our vibrations may be different, our form may change, but we are all part of the Universal Energy – part of all that exists. We are part of the whole energy of creation and embedded in the rest of existence.

There is no separation. You are part of one thing, an interconnected web of life, of energy that connects everything to everything else.

You are One with everything that exists.

---

[5] Gary Zukav, *The Dancing Wu Li Masters: An Overview of the New Physics*, page 72
[6] Gary Zukav, *The Dancing Wu Li Masters: An Overview of the New Physics*, page 179

Affirmation 3

The Source of My Creative Power

I am a part of the universal energy

The source of creation

The ultimate expression of being

Creation and Creator

It is what I AM

3

The Source of Your Creative Power

Through every star, through every blade of grass, is not
God made visible if we will only open our minds and eyes.
Thomas Carlyle (1795 – 1881)

Everything in our universe comes from the same energy, the same elements that came into existence when the universe was created. The energy that expanded and created everything we know still exists. It is all that exists - the total energy that encompasses everything in existence. It is the universal energy, the universal consciousness.

It is our source and the source of everything in existence. If there is nothing, no-thing, that is not part of the universal consciousness or energy – then everything is part of that universal energy, the animate, the inanimate, our world, the stars, the ocean, plants, animals and us. Everything.

What is this source? It is the creator, it is creation. Those who are spiritual or religious may call this creative energy "God", "Source" or "Creator".

There are many faiths and traditions with varying beliefs about the "Creator", but many have one thing in common, that the Creator is separate from us, above us and much better than us. Usually we have to do extraordinary feats to be worthy to come close to the creator. So many of us have been taught that we are separate from the "Creator" and only the special few can get close. We have been told that the "Creator" sits in judgement of us and has rules, punishes indiscretions and rewards good deeds. The implication is that there are some people who are better than others and only those who are deemed good enough can get close to the "Creator".

We need to change this view of ourselves as separate from the "Creator". If we are all part of one universal consciousness, part of one universal creative energy then how can we be separate from it? We are part of the universal whole. We are not separate from this universal creative energy, we are this creative energy. We are an integral part of the Source.

Why is it important to change our view of separation?

It is this view of "Creator" as separate from us that has led to a great deal of suffering in the world.

Almost daily on the news, we see the destruction of life caused by war and terrorism. Throughout history, many wars have been waged and incredible cruelty inflicted on people in the name of God, or another deity people believed in – sometimes even between those believing in different versions of the same faith. These conflicts are still happening now. No matter what the circumstances, each side believes they are right and the other side is wrong. Each side sees itself as separate to, and more righteous than the other side. Each believes that their "Creator" is on their side.

If we are all part of one universal creative consciousness, does this make sense? Why would the Universal Creator take sides? Why would the Creator of all of us, choose one group above another? That is like saying that part of your body is better than another and you can destroy that part - but destroying one part affects all of it.

It is our view of ourselves as separate from each other that leads us to judge and fear others. We see ourselves as more righteous or better than others - whether this feeling of superiority is about race, gender or status in society. This feeling of separation enables us to justify hurting someone else.

If we want peace in the world, we need to change this view of ourselves as separate. If we change our thinking and acknowledge and live in a way that accepts that everything in our universe is part of one whole and that every part affects the whole, the world we live in would be a very different place.

Our thinking matters.

Quantum physics is showing us not only that everything is energy but that there are indications that a single consciousness pervades the universe.[7] That every particle, every being, from atom to human, appears to contain a level of information, of conscious wisdom. This wisdom or idea then forms into the energy that we are made of. This implies that the source of creation is an underlying wisdom or idea and that thought may in fact be the basis of creation.

---

7 Gerald L Schroeder, *The Hidden Face of God: Science Reveals the Ultimate Truth*, Touchstone, New York, 2001, page 25

This book is about how quantum physics is showing that thought is the basis of creation and that there are indications that a single consciousness pervades the universe. Schroeder explains that every particle, every being, from atom to human, appears to contain a level of information, of conscious wisdom.

We originate from this thought energy, from the underlying universal wisdom and consciousness of the universe.

It doesn't matter what we call this underlying wisdom or thought energy. It is what we are.

We really are one. We are one with the universal creative energy. We are creators.

Affirmation 4

Who I Am

I know who I am

I am energy. I am Spirit

A vibration of energy consciousness

Part of the universal consciousness

An eternal oneness

I accept who I am without judgement

It is good to be me

I am a glorious being

4

Who Are You?

He who knows others is wise
He who knows himself is enlightened
Lao Tzu (c 6th century BC)

Who Are You?

It is a fundamental question. Who you believe you are determines your approach to life. Do you see yourself as a unique powerful individual or as someone dependent and reliant on others? How do you define yourself?

When asked who you are, do you state your name? That is often what is expected but your name does not explain who you are. It is a title usually given to you by someone else. You can change your name and many of us do, at various times of our lives. You may have a nickname, or take on a married name or change your name by deed poll. Your name is important but it does not explain who you are.

You might say that you are someone's brother, sister, mother or father, wife or husband, but this explains a relationship – who you are in relation to someone else. It is part of who you are, but only a small part.

You may define yourself by your occupation. You might say you are a student, a housewife, an office worker or doctor, but your occupation does not define who you are. It explains what you do at a particular point in time. Your occupation will change over time as you grow, develop, mature and retire.

Those who define themselves by their relationship with others or through their occupation often feel lost when the relationship or the occupation ends - like the mother who feels empty when her children grow up and leave home, or the person who always defined themselves through their job, retiring and feeling that they are now nobody.

None of these things explain who you are. Your name, your relationships, your occupation are the social you – who you are in your interaction with society. It explains a little of what you are but not who you are.

Who Are You?

Are you your body? Your body changes every day, you age and your cells are constantly being replaced. Our cells change at a rapid rate, dying and being renewed. You grow old, your appearance changes. Your physical body is a shell that contains you; it does not define you.

Are you your mind? You can change your mind and control your mind. You can decide what to think, do and act. You can decide how to react to the circumstances of your life. You have amazing intellectual capabilities, but this does not define you. You are more than your mind, more than your intellect.

You are an emotional being with a myriad of different feelings and emotions passing through you every day, but even this is not all you are. You can control your emotions. You can decide to be angry or to calm down. You are more than your emotions.

You are a social, intellectual, emotional and physical human being but this does not capture the essence of who you are. You are much more than this, something real, yet hard to define.

Who Are You?

At the core of your being you are spirit – a vibration of energy consciousness – and energy is eternal. The density and vibration of your energy may change when you take on a human existence. Your level of consciousness may change, but who you are at the core of your being remains. It is by acknowledging and getting in touch with the core of who you are that you can know the connection between all of us and the universal energy of our source.

By recognising who you are as spirit, and raising your level of awareness, your energy becomes lighter and the barriers between the human existence and the spiritual existence start to dissolve. Your creative power becomes greater as you get in touch with the creative energies of the universe. You begin to understand the interrelationship between everything that exists. Synchronicity starts to occur; your thoughts become more instantly creative.

You begin to more fully live who you are – a spiritual creative being who is a part of the creative universal energy, the universal spirit, the oneness of existence.

Affirmation 5

I Am a Creator

I am a creative being

I am conscious of who I am

My thoughts, my feelings

My choices, my actions

Create my present

Create my future

5

You Are a Creator

*We are what we think. All that we are arises with our thoughts.
With our thoughts, we make the world.*
Gautama Buddha (c563BCE–c483 BCE)

We are wonderful creations.

We are also creators. We are not passive observers of life but active participants in the creation of the future, not just of our lives but also of our world. The things we decide to do or not do shape our life and the lives of those around us.

We are more powerful than we realise.

Most of us go through life reacting to circumstances that happen to us without realising that we affect the future with every thought, every feeling and every action we take or do not take. You do this whether you are conscious of it or not.

You are creating your life and affecting all of existence with every thought, every choice and every action you take. Your thoughts are creative. In fact, thought is not only the basis of all creation – it is creation.

Quantum physics now suggests that thought may literally be the source of creation. That in fact, for all existence, there is "no-thing" there, that all of existence is really more a thought than a thing.[8] We are conscious beings, energy beings, and our influence extends further than we imagine.

Imagine how different your life would be – how different your attitude to life would be – if you lived consciously with the knowledge that every thought, every decision you make will influence your life, and the lives of those around you and even impact on the future of the world.

You might say, "Not me, I'm not that important", but you are.

Every moment of the day we make decisions that affect us, and the people around us. This happens on a physical level which we can see and be conscious of, but it also happens at the very core of our being – with every atom and sub-atomic particle that makes up our being. Our thoughts, actions, decisions and feelings are energy and every thought we have draws similar thought energies to it. These can change and affect the decisions and feelings of others, thereby creating the future of the world.

Quantum physics is now showing that we are connected and our energies interrelated. Quantum entanglement is the proven phenomenon where atomic-sized objects are connected and remain connected with instantaneous reactions to stimuli no matter how far away they are, even many miles.

---

8 Gerald L Schroeder, *The Hidden Face of God: Science Reveals the Ultimate Truth*, page 4

Albert Einstein called this "spooky action at a distance".[9] Some scientists now suggest that the universe is a single entangled object and that this explains why we have feelings of connection with loved ones, even at a distance - that our thoughts and minds may in fact be connected.[10]

This makes sense when we realise that we are part of the All That Is – part of the energy of creation. We are not separate from this energy – we are this creative energy. That is the essence of who and what we are. Above all else, we are creators.

We are all interrelated and connected. By changing our thoughts, feelings and decisions, we change our future and the future of the world.

Change your thoughts and you change your outcome.

Knowing this, you can decide to consciously create your future and the life you want. If you want a crystal ball into your future, look inside yourself today.

---

9 Dean Radin, *Entangled Minds: Extrasensory Experiences in a Quantum Reality*, Paraview Pocket Books, New York, 2006, page 1.

This book is about how quantum entanglement shows us that our universe is one interconnected whole. Dean Radin uses this to show that psychic ability is real and can be based on scientific evidence.
10 Dean Radin, *Entangled Minds: Extrasensory Experiences in a Quantum Reality*, page 2.

Affirmation 6

I Trust My Intuition

I listen to my inner voice

It is there to guide me

It is my creative power within

It is my connection to the whole

6

Trust Your Intuition

What lies behind us and what lies before us are tiny matters compared to what lies within us.
Ralph Waldo Emerson (1803 – 1882)

You are an incredible being.

At your core you are spirit and have a connection to the universal spirit, the universal consciousness. You are literally a part of universal creative energy. You are therefore never alone. There is the voice inside you that knows and guides your decisions – if only you listen to it.

What is that voice?

Partly it is your conscious mind – your set of values that you have built up through your experiences that assist you in judging things that happen to you, or in determining the decisions you make. It is your belief system of what is right and wrong.

But there is something else. We can all feel it. It is the voice that tells you something that doesn't always make logical sense, but you know that it is right. It is your intuition, your gut feeling. It is a knowing.

It's the inner voice inside you that warns you and protects you. It is the part of you that is connected to the whole. At our core we are connected and it is this connection, this intuition that is there to guide you.

Have you ever been in a new situation or met someone new and instantly got a feeling about him or her – either a positive feeling or a feeling that warns you to stay away, that something is not right? That is your intuition at work.

Have you had times when you heard your inner voice and ignored it, only to find that what your inner voice was telling you has become reality? Your intuition is the feeling to do something or act in a way that may not be logical or make sense but that deep down you know is right.

Sometimes, we try to block that inner voice and avoid listening to it. Sometimes this voice gets clouded by other things that are happening in our lives, or by other people's expectations that we take on as our own. We often don't trust our own feelings and intuition. We only need to stop and listen to our own self-talk to realise that it is often far from positive. Our self-talk is often like, "I can't get anything right", "I'm an idiot", or "Why on earth did I do that?". We are often our worst critics.

We underestimate ourselves constantly. We rarely trust ourselves to make the right decision about something. Usually we ask others what they think. There is nothing wrong with getting another's opinion, provided the decision we make is what feels right for us.

Often we make decisions that don't feel right – whether this is succumbing to peer pressure or other people's expectations or what we think we should do rather than what we feel is right in the core of our being.

Not following your own intuition is like fighting and blocking yourself and your own creative power. If something feels wrong, or makes you feel uncomfortable, or guilty, then trust that feeling.

Inside each of us is our connection to spirit, to the universal energy of creation. If we recognise this and trust the core of our being – trust our intuition – the creative power we have will be greatly enhanced. Look for signs and coincidences. The more you are guided by your inner voice the more synchronicity you will create.

Whether you believe this intuition is your inner self, your higher self or maybe your guide or angel talking with you – it doesn't matter.

Follow your heart and intuition. It is your creative power within.

Affirmation 7

Imagination

My imagination is a wonderful thing

It is energy set into motion

I imagine it

I believe it

I create it

7

Imagination

*Imagination is the beginning of creation.
You imagine what you desire, you will what you imagine
and at last you create what you will.*
George Bernard Shaw (1856 – 1950)

Thought is the basis of everything we do, all of our actions. It is the start of the creative process.

The process of creation is to first think it, then speak it and then do it.[11] Creation begins with thought, with knowing. Before anything can become a reality in physical form, it has to become a reality in thought.

Everything that man has created has come into being because someone first thought about it and imagined the possibilities. We first have to think it, then we have to believe it is possible and only then can we create it.

---
11 Neale Donald Walsch, *Conversations with God: An Uncommon Dialogue Book 1,* page 91

Thoughts are energy. Our imagination and intention put that energy into motion. Imagination is your thoughts in action. It is your creative power in motion. Through your imagination you can fly and reach the rainbow, travel to the stars, or be the best player at the football match – there is nothing that you can't do in your imagination.

Imagination allows us to go beyond our material reality. It allows us to explore other realities and ways of being. It allows us to tap into our soul and our senses and to create endless possibilities in our mind. There are no limits and you have total control over what you imagine.

When you imagine something vividly, your body reacts as if what you imagine is actually happening. Scientific researchers now believe that imagining imitates real sensory perception.[12] When you imagine something, the visual cortex in your brain lights up – just as if you were experiencing a real event. This research suggests that your brain cannot tell the difference between a real experience and something that you vividly imagine and your body also reacts accordingly, changing your physiology and reacting in similar ways to actual events and things that you vividly imagine.

You imagine happy, wonderful things and you feel happy, uplifted and you feel like you can do anything. Even the chemicals in your body react. Your thoughts change your physiology.

The effect of stress on health is well known and has a significant impact on health and well being. You imagine sad, hurtful things and that is also how you feel – depressed, your body slumps

---

[12] "The Feeling of Colour", *New Scientist*, vol. 185, no. 2484, 29 January 2005, Reed Business Information, Sydney Australia, page 41.

This article explores the idea that colour is one of the many senses we have in addition to the five senses we know about of hearing, sight, taste, smell and touch. It mentions that scientific researchers now believe that the visual cortex in our brain activates the same way whether we imagine something or actually see it. This research suggests that our body reacts in similar ways to actual events and things that we imagine.

and your stress levels increase. Cell biologist, Bruce Lipton, contends that our thoughts activate changes in our cells, our hormones, our membranes and that these changes affect our health and well being. We are not victims of our genes, we are in control through our subconscious and our thoughts.[13] Our beliefs and our subconscious programming, both positive and negative, control our biology,[14] and knowing this we can change our thinking to improve our physical health as well as our happiness.

We program our subconscious. The subconscious mind acts like a pre-programmed, goal driven mechanism, delivering the goals set by the conscious mind. You program your subconscious every day with repetitions of your thoughts and feelings and by the experiences you have. Your thoughts matter.

We can choose to change our subconscious programming through our conscious thoughts, our imagination. Imagination is our thoughts in action. We can use our imagination to create the life we really want for ourselves. What we think about and imagine, we can create.

Realise how powerful your imagination and your thoughts are. Your self-talk, your thoughts about yourself and other people, your thoughts about what you can achieve and what you believe you can't do are the driving force for what happens in your life. If your thoughts and imagination are negative, you can decide to change them.

They are your thoughts, your imagination and therefore, your choice.

---

13 Bruce Lipton, *Biology of Belief: Unleashing the Power of Consciousness, Matter & Miracles*, Mountain of Love/Elite Books, Santa Rosa USA, 2005, page 27.

In this book, Bruce Lipton, a cell biologist, states that our lives are not ruled by our genes but by our membranes that are influenced by our own thoughts.

14 Bruce Lipton, Biology of Belief: Unleashing the Power of Consciousness, Matter & Miracles, page 30.

If you imagine it and then believe and know that it can happen, then it most likely will happen. If you think you can't do something, then you most likely can't do it.

If you believe you can do something, and know you can do it, then your creative power becomes manifest.

Affirmation 8

I Have the Freedom to Choose

I am

Free to choose

My thoughts and feelings

My attitudes and my responses

No-one can take this away from me

It is my ultimate freedom

8

Freedom to Choose

We choose our joy and sorrows
long before we experience them.
Kahlil Gibran (1883 – 1931)

Your greatest freedom is your ability to choose.

You choose what to think, say, do and imagine. Every decision you make is a choice. No one can take these choices away from you.

Every day you make choices. Even when you don't make a decision but allow things to happen to you, you are making a choice – a choice not to decide. Everything you do or don't do has consequences. Every action has a reaction. Every cause has an effect. Even a decision to do nothing has a consequence. There is a matrix of possibilities and future consequences as a result of your choices. This means that many possible futures are open to you as a result of the choices you make.

Choosing to think a certain way, choosing an action or behaviour, in fact any choice you make is like choosing between two paths of the road. Each choice will take you to a different place. Once you have made the first choice, this will lead to other choices. At any point on the journey, you can decide what direction you will take, what road you will travel on. Each choice changes and creates your future and the future for everyone. Some of your choices may have a minor impact; other choices may have an enormous impact. Your choices affect many people around you, now and into the future. They create the future.

Sometimes, things may happen to us that we feel we have no control over, but even in the most horrific of circumstances, once trauma and shock have subsided, we still decide how we respond to and feel about the circumstance we find ourselves in. We are always free to choose how we respond to the situations of our lives. Even if your physical freedom is taken away from you, no-one can take away your freedom to choose how you will react to your circumstances.

How many times have you said, "He made me do it", "It was her fault", "I couldn't help it", or "He made me angry"? We all say this – thinking, "I'm not to blame" – but all this does is give our personal power to someone else. If someone makes you feel bad it is because you are allowing them to do so. It leaves us with seemingly no control over our lives, with the feeling that we are at the mercy of others.

Blaming others is refusing to acknowledge that you do have the freedom to choose how you will respond. Others might try to make you feel small, hurt you with words or actions – but no one can make you feel good or bad. Only you can do that. It is always your choice – even if we sometimes find it easier to not take responsibility, even if the choices are not easy ones.

Only you can decide how you react and respond to something – no-one else can decide what you will feel or think. Realising this gives you freedom – gives you power. Personal power is the power you have over your thoughts, your mind and your feelings and therefore, your power to create your life. It is the power to view things the way you choose to.

This is your ultimate freedom. No-one can take away your power to choose how you feel and respond to something. Through this power comes your power to create. Thoughts and feelings are the basis of creation and you have complete control over your thoughts and feelings.

No-one can make you choose what your attitude will be.

The choice is yours.

Affirmation 9

My Attitude Matters

My attitude and thinking are energies

that attract like energy

I am conscious of what I am attracting

I attract the energies that serve me

I am in control

9

Your Attitude Matters

*The greatest discovery of our generation is that human beings can alter their lives by altering their attitudes of mind.
As you think, so shall you be.*
William James (1842 – 1910)

Your attitude draws things to you. Your choices, imagination, thoughts and therefore your attitude are forms of energy that create the consequences and circumstances of your life.

Have there been times in your life when you have felt happy and positive, and everything seemed to be going your way? Or times when you were down and feeling miserable and nothing seemed to go right? This occurs because energy attracts like energy. Your thoughts and attitude are energies that create your outcomes. The universe presents infinite possibilities and it will reflect back to you what you are feeling and what you are thinking and doing. You will attract like energies to your feelings and attitude, creating the outcome of your thoughts.

Most of the time, we are not conscious or aware of what we are attracting into our lives. We focus on the day, the problem at hand, the money we need, the people we don't like, never realising that by focusing on all of these negative aspects of our lives, we are attracting more of that very negativity into our lives. Like attracts like.

If you don't like what is happening in your life, then you need to look at your own attitude to life – the thoughts you have about who you are and the circumstances surrounding your life. Are your thoughts supporting the kind of life you would like to create or are they doing the opposite? What is your attitude to yourself, others or what is happening in your life? Is it positive or negative?

This is why our thoughts, our self-talk and our innermost feelings about something are so important. A single thought may not have much of an impact, but if we keep thinking the same way, we create an accumulation of energy and begin to create what we imagine and think about, whether it is positive or negative. The universe will assist by attracting like energy to your thoughts. You literally attract particular possibilities to you.

If you believe that good things never happen to you, then that is the experience you will create. If you believe you are not worthy and not good enough, that is what you will create. You will draw from the universe what you believe and what you expect.

Have you ever thought that you keep attracting the same type of person in your life, the same type of relationships that never quite work? Think about why you are attracting these people to you. What are your feelings about yourself? Do you believe you will never find the right person or that somehow you don't deserve it? Be conscious of your feelings, actions and words. I've heard people who are yearning for a relationship say things like, "I don't think I will ever meet the right person", and then they are upset that they never do.

The universe brings to you what you tell it to. Positivity will bring positive outcomes; negativity will bring negative outcomes. If you want to change your life and the consequences you are creating, you need to affirm the positive outcomes you want. To change your life you need to change your thoughts and attitude by replacing them with different ones. You need to affirm the new things you want in your life as if you already have them. You may not believe it at first, but repeating new positive thoughts (energy) draws like positive energy to you.

If you know what you want to create in your life, then you can use your thoughts to create it. It is your attitude to life – how you feel about your life and the circumstances you find yourself in that determines the quality of your life. You choose how and what you think and what you think determines your choices. No matter what your circumstances, it is your attitude that affects your happiness and your attitude is your choice.

Change your attitude, change your thoughts and you change your outcome.

Affirmation 10

I Choose Consciously

My choices create my future

I am aware of the choices I make

And the consequences of my choices

I determine the direction of my life

I choose consciously

10

Conscious Choice

I find the great thing in this world is not so much where we stand, as in what direction we are moving: To reach the port of heaven, we must sail sometimes with the wind and sometimes against it, but we must sail, and not drift, nor lie at anchor.
Oliver Wendell Holmes, Snr (1809 – 1894)

You choose consciously or unconsciously, every day, in every moment of your life.

Any choice, whether conscious or unconscious is a creative force. However, to truly embrace your creative power, you need to consciously choose what you think, feel and do.

One of the hardest, yet most empowering things to do is to take responsibility for your choices and the outcome of those choices. We are responsible for our choices whether we are conscious of them or not. Conscious choosing means understanding that a choice has consequences and that in making the choice you accept the responsibility for the consequences as well. It takes courage to do this but doing so enables you to be in control of the creative process and to deliberately create your outcomes.

You own your decisions. You own your consequences. You are responsible for the choices and the outcome whether you wish to accept the responsibility or not. Conscious choosing means being aware that your choices have consequences and that even though you may not foresee the full extent and implications of your actions and decisions, you know that your choices have brought you there.

Being aware of the consequences allows you to be conscious of the possible future you will create. Choosing consciously allows you to direct your creative power.

Even the simplest choice, such as whether to catch a train or drive, stay home or go out, can have enormous consequences for your future. Every day we make choices that can totally change the direction of our lives. You decide to help someone, or save someone from a near fatal accident. You can change the course of your life and the life of so many others. You make a decision to leave a place early and are involved in an accident or narrowly miss having an accident because of the choice you made. Think about your choice of which career to undertake. How different would your life be if you made another choice? You meet someone and they become your friend, partner or spouse. You may have children together. How different would the world be if that event hadn't occurred, if you had made a different decision?

Choosing consciously allows you to become the director in your life instead of someone under the apparent direction of others. It allows you to decide which path you want to take in your life and to change direction if you wish.

When you make your choices unconsciously, not taking into account the possible consequences, allowing things to happen to you, it is like choosing to allow your boat to drift at the mercy of the elements. Doing this is choosing to allow others and external circumstances to dictate what happens next. This choice is neither right nor wrong – it is simply your choice, and it's a choice we may make at times, but it is not an empowering choice.

Choosing consciously means making decisions about the direction you are going and deciding to take the journey, to move along the road of life. Sometimes we don't always foresee the consequences of our choices. It may not work out exactly how we want, but we can always learn from our choices and change direction if we want.

Being aware of possible outcomes and taking responsibility for those outcomes empowers you to be able to make a different choice if you wish. Accepting the responsibility that goes with choice can be difficult, but it is enormously empowering. It means that you can be consciously in control of your creative power.

It means you can direct your life, creating your life, fully aware that the choices you make create your future. Taking responsibility for your choices and their consequences enables you to create your future consciously. It means sailing, not drifting.

I hope you sail.

Affirmation 11

I Am True to Myself

I am true to who I am

I follow my heart

It is the key to my soul

To my power within

I know myself

I understand myself

I listen to myself

I listen to my power within

11

Dare to Be Yourself

Who looks outside, dreams; who looks inside, awakes.
Carl Jung (1875 - 1961)

There are very few of us who would say that they did not want to be true to themselves, but how many of us really know what that means? How many of us truly know ourselves, know exactly why we do what we do or truly understand our own feelings?

Sometimes it is easier for us to surrender our true feelings, to pretend to be something else in order to please friends, peer groups or people we love. If we don't know who we are, what we believe in and what is important to us, then it is easy to succumb to group pressure and sometimes do things we may not be comfortable with.

To fully embrace your personal power and your personal strength, you need to follow your feelings. If you are doing something that does not make you feel good, then you are cheating yourself, not being true to who you are.

To know ourselves we need to go inside. We need to explore our feelings, our attitudes, our values but we need to do this without judgement. To know ourselves, we initially need to become an observer of the things we do and feel.

Observe yourself; look at the way you react with other people. Look at the way you react in different circumstances. Observe without judgement. When you do or say something, stop and think why you did that – not from the point of view of judging whether what you did was the "right" or "wrong" thing – but simply to understand yourself better. Do you act the same way with everyone? Very few of us do. We often show different parts of ourselves to different people.

Observe all of this without judgement – but question it. Why do you act or feel a certain way? Is it out of love or fear? Is it because you want to be accepted? If someone annoys you, think why that is. Are there parts of yourself that you always keep hidden? If so, why?

Look at your job. Is it something that you love to do? Why are you doing it? What stops you from doing something else? What does it tell you about your values? It may be fear that is stopping you, or wanting to provide for your family, or it may be simply that you don't know what you would like to do. The important thing is to ask the questions and to observe without judgement. It often takes courage to really look at our reasons and motivations for doing things but it is by looking at ourselves honestly that we get to know ourselves and begin to discover what truly brings us joy, happiness and purpose.

Look objectively at all aspects of you and your life. What are the things you value more than anything else? What do you love about yourself and about others? How do you feel? Are there things you don't like? Are there things you want to change? If you didn't have to worry about money or doing what you felt others wanted or needed you to do, what would you be doing? Once you find this, is there any way of including more of what you want to do in your life?

You reveal yourself to others through your behaviour. The way you discover yourself is through looking objectively at the thoughts and feelings that drive your behaviour. Often we even try to fool ourselves about things we have done, said or thought. Go deep inside you. Discover who you are – at the very heart of your soul, for in doing so, you discover the core of who you are.

When you look at your life, your feelings and your actions objectively you become an observer. Who is the observer? The observer is really the essence of who you are - the spiritual you, your higher self, your connection with spirit. You are the observer – you are not what is being observed.

You are spirit on a journey and your body, your life, your circumstances, your friends, this lifetime, are all part of that journey. You are the participant and creator of your journey. Know who you are and the journey you have chosen and created for yourself. Observe what you have created and why. Live the journey you have chosen to experience in this lifetime.

Know the essence of who you are.

Know yourself. Be yourself.

Affirmation 12

My Feelings are a Key to My Soul

My feelings are my own

I embrace them

I accept them

I learn from them

My feelings are a key to my soul

12

Embrace Your Feelings

Eyes that do not cry, do not see.
Swedish Proverb

Your feelings are a way of knowing yourself.

Don't deny your feelings and emotions. Embrace them. We often tend to hide our feelings or believe that we shouldn't feel the way we do, that it is wrong to feel sad or feel angry. It's only from experiencing sorrow, that we can know joy. Only by experiencing pain can we know pleasure. Often, it is by surviving the difficult times that we grow and become stronger, more empowered individuals.

What makes you feel wonderful, what brings you joy, laughter and fulfillment? What causes you to feel angry, sad or unhappy? It is through acknowledging your feelings that they become a means for you to learn more about yourself. It is a way of finding out who you are.

We all have the right to feel the way we do. Your feelings are your own. No-one can make you feel a certain way.

To empower yourself means being honest with yourself and being honest about how you feel and why you are feeling it. We often blame others for the way we feel. We will often say things like: he made me angry; she made me sad or she makes me happy; or he made me feel wonderful. No-one can make us feel anything unless we allow them to.

Your feelings are just that – yours. You control them – they are your reactions.

Anger is something that we almost always blame on others, but it is not other people that cause our anger. Sometimes our anger comes from a sense of injustice or injury. Sometimes, it is our unmet expectations of people that cause our anger. We expect people to behave perfectly on the road, and get angry when they don't. We expect everyone to listen to us when we want them to, and get angry when they don't. We expect our children to always do what we say, when we say it, and we get angry when they don't. We expect everything to go the way we want it and get angry when it doesn't.

Whether or not we feel that our anger is justified, the feeling of anger, as with all of our other feelings, is a choice we make. All our feelings are choices we are making – usually unconscious choices and reactions. Sometimes our reactions have been programmed in us from when we were young and we are barely aware that we are reacting in a certain way.

Our feelings give us an opportunity to know more about ourselves. Your feelings are a way of exploring who you are and the issues you may need to deal with. Why does something make you angry, why do you feel sad, what gives you pleasure? What is at the core of these feelings? Being conscious of your feelings and the fact that they are choices you make empowers you to learn more about yourself and to choose to feel differently, if you wish.

Your feelings are powerful. It is how you feel about something that often determines the outcome. Your feelings have enormous creative power. They are an energy that affects not only you, but also others around you.

Embrace your feelings – explore your feelings – they are a key to your soul. A key to finding out who you really are.

Affirmation 13

I Learn from my Fears

There is no need to fear my fears

They are an opportunity

To know myself

To understand myself

They offer an opportunity to grow

Love can overcome fear

I can overcome fear

I choose to love

13

Understand Your Fears

Courage is resistance to fear, mastery of fear - not absence of fear.
Mark Twain (1835 – 1910)

Don't fear your fears – understand your fears. Think about your fear. What is it that you are really scared of? What does it tell you about yourself? What would you really love to do if you had no fear?

It's okay to feel fear. You are never going to be totally without fear, but don't let it scare you.

The feeling of fear is your mind trying to protect you from a potentially dangerous situation. That can be a very good thing if you are in danger and need to avoid getting physically hurt. Fear also arises when you a faced with a new situation or a different set of circumstances. Your mind is giving you a warning that something is unknown, you are not sure what the consequences will be so you need to tread carefully, so the fear response is activated.

The key is to recognise the difference between feeling fear because you are in physical danger and your life at risk or just feeling fear of the unknown consequences.

Sometimes the biggest fear is change. We all have a comfort zone but often the comfort zone we are in is not very comfortable; however, it is familiar. Fear of the unknown, fear of change often keeps us in a familiar zone which is far from comfortable and sometimes even painful. Change can be scary but change brings the potential for growth and new possibilities.

Some people fear failure and avoid doing things for fear that they will not succeed – not realising that this effectively achieves the very thing that they fear. Some people fear success – fearing that it may change their lives and as a result do nothing and may lose incredible opportunities and live with regret later on.

Some may avoid new relationships because they have been hurt in the past and no longer want to be hurt. That is understandable and fear of being emotionally hurt again is a strong motivator. Staying with this fear and not taking the risk to be hurt means missing out on the possibility of a wonderful, loving and fulfilling relationship.

You may want to do something you fear, but put it off thinking, "I will do it when I stop feeling fearful." Avoiding what you fear will not make the fear go away. In many ways it will make the fear increase because you spend more time in the fear and attach further energy and negativity to your fears.

You may simply avoid the things that you fear, thinking that you will then avoid feeling fear. We fear the feeling of fear. Some of us even feel that we are somehow lacking because we may fear things others don't fear at all.

Fear is not something to avoid. It is something to explore. It provides an incredible opportunity for growth and for a greater understanding of yourself.

The best way to overcome fear is to do the very thing that you fear. When you do this, your fear may simply disappear. You often realise that your fears were unwarranted or overestimated. How wonderful do you feel when you overcome a fear and succeed? By overcoming fear, you personally empower yourself as a stronger person, in control of your circumstances and your outcomes.

Even if you choose not to do the things you fear, you can choose to explore your fear and look at what it tells you about yourself. Sometimes our fears are an indicator of other feelings we have about ourselves or others.

What is the essence of your fear? What is the cause of your fear? Approach your fear with love. This will also empower you as it gives you a greater understanding of yourself and your feelings. You can then make conscious choices rather than be at the mercy of your own fears.

The opposite of fear is love. Fear is at the heart of much of the violence in the world. Many people think that war, racism and sexism are based on hatred, and superficially they could be, but the basis of that hatred is almost always fear. Fear that there is a lack or shortage of resources that we must fight to keep for ourselves. Fear that if we allow others of different culture, race or sex into our home, our country or our workplace, that somehow they will take over from us and our way of life. Fear that if we don't win, it means that we will lose. Fear that if we don't strike first, we will be struck down. Fear that the universe will not provide enough for everyone.

Fear breeds fear, unless we stop and look objectively at what we fear. When you hate something, look at the object of your hatred and try to determine what it is that you fear as the basis of that hatred. The reality is that there is enough and this is found not through fear, but through love.

Love yourself and understand your fear. Don't be critical of yourself that you feel fear. Thank your fear. After all, it is a safety mechanism - your mind trying to keep you safe. Explore your fears; are they stopping you from achieving something you have always wanted to do? Are your fears of getting hurt stopping you from taking a risk with a new relationship? Consciously decide what you want to do.

You can choose to empower yourself. You can feel the fear and act anyway to achieve your goals, try new things, undertake new adventures and watch the possibilities unfold.

Affirmation 14

I Break the Ties That Bind Me

I break the ties that hurt me

I break the ties that bind me

I forgive

It is for me

For my freedom

I free myself

14

Recognise the Ties That Bind

I will permit no man to narrow and degrade my soul by making me hate him.
Booker T. Washington (1856 – 1915)

We are connected to everything in existence.

It is natural that those connections become stronger between us and the people, animals and even things that we are close to. Sometimes those connections are strengthened to the point that they become "ties" - we almost literally become bound to them.

This is a very positive experience when we love someone or something. Our ties to our partners, children, family, friends and even our pets can be incredibly strong and powerful. Sometimes we even have a sense of when our loved ones are happy or in danger and can literally feel the ties binding us to those that are close to us.

Sometimes, we only recognise these ties when we break off relationships or our loved one dies. Our connection with others can often be so close that we feel like part of us has also died when the relationship ends through separation or death. Our connections to those we love are positive and often empowering. It is something to savour and nurture.

Not all ties to others are positive. Even our language indicates that we are aware of ties we can have with people and that sometimes these ties need to be severed. When we want to break off a relationship that no longer is serving us, we often use expressions such as "I need to break it off", "I need to cut the ties", "I feel bound in that relationship". These are a recognition that, sometimes, the ties we have to people can become suffocating. It is not always easy to break off ties we have with others and even with things – how hard is it to break addictions?

When a connection becomes bondage, it is not serving us any more and we need to sever the connection – to let go. One of the more destructive ties is to choose to remain bound to things or people that hurt you. It is a choice. People can hurt you physically or emotionally, but you choose the way you will react to what has happened. You can choose to dwell on the hurt, bind it to you with thoughts of anger or revenge or you can choose to let it go. The way to let go and cut the ties with people who have hurt you is to forgive them.

To forgive and let go of anger or resentment does not mean you are saying that what happened to you wasn't hurtful – just that you choose not to continue letting it hurt you. Gautama Buddha is known to have said that holding on to anger is like taking poison and expecting the other person to die.

Some people who have been hurt may hold on to their hurt, anger, hatred or bitterness for years, even sometimes after the person who hurt them has died. The only person they are hurting is themselves.

Who are you hurting by holding on to your hurt – the other person? Or yourself? We have all been hurt, but it is our choice whether we stay tied to that hurt or not.

To forgive is not something you do for someone else. It is something you give yourself. It is saying that you have been hurt enough and that you will not let that person or thing harm you anymore. It is cutting the ties between you and the person who hurt you. It is saying – I win, not them. It is to let go of the negativity, of the negative energy that can only bring more negativity to you. Forgiving gives you peace of mind.

Remember, like attracts like. If you hold bitterness and frustration inside you, then you are strengthening the bond and connection between you and the person who hurt you and you are more likely to attract more bitterness and anger into your life. It won't affect the person who you feel harmed you. It will affect only you.

To forgive does not mean that someone who hurt you goes unpunished. What happens to them as a consequence of their actions is a totally separate issue, but one for them to deal with. Forgiving means cutting the ties. You do it for yourself. You do it to cut the ties that bind you to that event or that person. Being bound to another person or event will never make you free. It will hold you back from living, from fully expressing and being the person you were born to be.

Equally, you need to forgive yourself. If you feel that you have not done or achieved something you should have, or have done things you are unhappy about - forgive yourself. Break the ties with the negativity about yourself you are holding on to. You can then be free to create new circumstances in your life, to make new choices and change direction.

Unbind yourself, forgive others and forgive yourself. Keep the connections that enhance and empower you and cut the ties with the rest.

Free yourself.

Affirmation 15

Being

I experience the moment

I experience life with a sense of wonder

I am present in the moment

I Be

I AM

15

Being

May you live all the days of your life.
Jonathan Swift (1667 – 1745)

Too often we are rushing around trying to do many things at once, thinking about all the things we didn't do and the things we still have to do. We are usually so busy *doing*, that we spend very little time *being*.

To be, we need to stop doing. Being is stillness – it is timeless. One way of coming close to this state of being is to live in the moment. It is through being that we come close to experiencing the true nature of who we are.

None of us really knows what will happen in the next moment. We can guess, and most of the time we will be right, but we all know of events of nature, accidents or deliberate actions by man that have happened in a moment and have changed people's lives forever.

Being can only be done now. It is not a past or future state. We usually spend most of the time worrying about the past (which we can't change) or possible future outcomes (which may or may not occur) instead of living in the present and making decisions to bring about the future we want.

All we really have is now.

Many times I have wished my life away and heard others say similar things. "I can't wait until Friday", "I wish today was over", and "I can't wait until the holidays". Thinking this way implies a powerlessness to affect the way we feel now. It implies a hope that the future has to be better than the present, that we are unhappy with what is occurring now and looking forward to a time when we will be happy – the weekend, the holiday, when we are home.

But, happiness is not a future event; living is not a future event. Living happens now.

When we focus on now, we see the world as the wonder it is. We really live our lives. Everything becomes special, the magnificence of nature, the flowers, the plants, animals, and the people you are with.

When we stop trying to get through life, to get through the day and just stop and experience the moment, the whole world becomes a different place. Time stands still and even the most mundane things seem wonderful. You see things that you normally don't pay attention to. You become calmer and the stress decreases. Problems diminish when what you focus on is literally each second of time – without worrying or thinking about what comes next.

Being and living in the moment means getting in touch with who you are. When you are being, time seems to stand still. Past, present and future become one when we are experiencing who we are. Being allows you to experience the wonder of the present moment.

There are also many health benefits. Being mindful, whether through meditation, the practice of stillness or being fully immersed in the now moment, reduces stress, relieves anxiety, is relaxing and energising.

When we stop doing and are being, we not only recognise the connection with all of creation – we live the connection. Existing through each day is not the same as living each day.

It is in being that we are truly ourselves.

Being is also the key to creating the future you want. The future is created in the present. Your future is created now. Your present thoughts, feelings and actions are what collapse future possibilities into your future reality. You attract like energies into your life through what you are thinking, feeling and choosing right now.

Live now. Live today. Find the wonder of life.

Affirmation 16

I Am Grateful

I am grateful for everything I have

I look at my life positively and I am thankful

Everyday there are more things to be grateful for

I foster an attitude of gratitude

I feel joy

16

Gratitude

Gratitude bestows reverence, allowing us to encounter everyday epiphanies, those transcendent moments of awe that change forever how we experience life and the world.
John Milton (1608 – 1674)

It is easy to focus on the negatives. So often we are unhappy, dissatisfied with our lives, our work and bodies. Every day we are bombarded with images about how we should look, what we should be buying, what the ideal job, house and family should look like. It is often difficult to avoid comparing ourselves to the images we see or the ideals that society portrays, and more often than not, those comparisons are negative. This can lead to low self esteem, and even more negative thoughts, causing more dissatisfaction and unhappiness.

It is easy to say, "stop the comparisons, be satisfied with what you have" but happiness and fulfillment does not come from "settling" for what you have, or from focusing on what you don't have. Happiness comes from being truly grateful for what you do have.

Gratitude is joyous and there are so many things to be grateful for. The fact that you are alive is a wondrous thing. You have the opportunity everyday to live, interact with others, interact with nature and have the possibility of change if you wish. Be grateful for being able to breathe fresh air and have water to drink and food to eat. Be grateful that you are able to read this book and able to write and express your ideas. Be grateful for the senses you have that enable you to experience the world. Be grateful for the people or animals in your life. Be grateful that you can experience the beauty of nature.

There might be things that you are not totally happy with. There may be the job you do not like or the people that cause you distress or the health problem that is debilitating, but there is always something to be grateful for if you remain positive. The job you don't like provides the money that enables you to buy food and have shelter. The people you don't like may help you grow and teach you more about yourself. The health issue may cause you to adjust your lifestyle and make different choices which in the long run, are positive.

Gratitude is an attitude of positivity. Being grateful for what you have and reinforcing this daily, by expressing what you are grateful for in life, focuses on positive experiences. As gratitude, like everything else, is energy, it attracts positive energies.

Being grateful does not mean that you cease to strive for change in your life. You may still want to improve your health, get a better job, have a bigger house or travel more. Being grateful for what you have and approaching your life from a positive perspective often provides the energy to be more open to opportunities and making changes. A positive perspective on life improves physical health and wellbeing, reduces stress and increases energy and happiness.

Taking the first steps to developing an attitude of gratitude can be as simple as every day committing to writing down or thinking about three things that you are grateful for and expanding on this until gratitude becomes a natural approach to life. When you step outside in the morning, be grateful for the sunshine or the rain that provides water. Be grateful for the clothes that keep you warm, for the roads and public transport that take you to your destination. The opportunity for being thankful for what you have in your life is always there.

Once you start thinking about life from the perspective of gratitude, joy will follow.

Affirmation 17

I Choose Happiness

Happiness is a way of being

I embrace the wonder of the moment

I am grateful for every moment

I am grateful for everything I do and have

I live fully and completely

I am happy

17

Choose Happiness

The foolish person seeks happiness in the distance;
The wise person grows it under his feet.
James Oppenheim (1882 – 1932)

We often hear about the pursuit of happiness or the search for happiness as if happiness existed "out there" for us to find. You will never find happiness in this way.

Sometimes we treat happiness as a future event - something to be achieved when we succeed in getting what we want. We believe that we will be happy when we have the right relationship, when we win the lottery, have that better job, go on that holiday or when we retire. There are so many future events we believe will bring us happiness when and if we achieve them. These things can certainly bring pleasure and satisfaction but happiness is a different thing. It is not something to gain after we have achieved a particular goal.

Happiness is not a destination. It is not a future event. It can only be experienced in the moment. It is a way of being.

Happiness is not dependent on material gain or external circumstances. The poorest person can be happy and the richest person can be miserable and unfulfilled. Wealth and possessions do not bring happiness.

Many times we allow our happiness to be dependent on other people or external events. We feel happy if someone does or says something that pleases us or we allow our happiness to be dependent on material gain or achievement. Happiness that is based on external gratification will never be long lasting.

Happiness is not the same as pleasure. There can be pleasure or pain from events in your life but happiness is a way of approaching life – a way of being, of accepting whatever happens and finding the positive in our experiences. External circumstances can definitely impact on your happiness. There are many situations in life, especially loss, pain and ill health that can impact on your feeling of happiness in the short term, but whether these circumstances have a lasting impact on your happiness is up to you.

The Dalai Lama teaches that once our basic needs such as food, shelter and clothing are met, it is our mind and attitude that are the key to happiness.[15] Everything we do is motivated by our desire for happiness. What we do every day and the choices we make are usually linked to either achieving immediate happiness or the hope for future happiness.

Finding inner happiness is also finding the positive energy within. The happier we feel the more energetic we feel. Happiness

---

15. His Holiness the 14th Dalai Lama and Howard C. Cutler, *The Art of Happiness: A Handbook for Living*, Hodder Australia, 1998, page 37.

In this book, The Dalai Lama shares how he achieved his own serenity and how we can find the same inner peace. He shows how to overcome depression, anxiety, anger and jealousy and that no matter the external circumstances, having a greater peace of mind enhances happiness in everyday life.

increases energy levels and increases health. Happiness releases endorphins, the hormone that reduces stress and makes us feel good.

Happiness is a state of acceptance and joy of living. It is an internal state – it is an attitude, a way you decide to be, regardless of what is happening to you. Happiness is to be in the now and to find joy and wonder in the moment. It is to live your life fully appreciating each moment. Happiness can only be achieved in the moment. Happiness is also feeling that we are doing and being our best. It is very difficult to be happy if you feel you are short selling yourself in some way.

Happiness is being true to who you are and what you believe in and being grateful for the wonderful moment of life. Gratitude brings happiness. When we are happy we are more likely to love, not only ourselves, but others. The Dalai Lama teaches that being kind and showing compassion will actually bring you happiness.[16] He goes further to state that the purpose of life is in fact, happiness.[17]

Most of us certainly are happier when we have a goal to achieve and a sense of purpose to life. When you are doing something that makes your heart sing and that you are passionate about, you are usually happy. It is a key motivator for the choices and decisions we make and key to understanding who we are.

If happiness is our purpose then perhaps it is so because to fully live our lives and to do this with happiness and joy means to live in the present and to feel grateful for life and all it brings.

Happiness is internal. It is a way of being and is only achieved in the present moment. Happiness is not "out there", it is in you. It is your choice.

---

16 His Holiness the 14th Dalai Lama and Howard C. Cutler, *The Art of Happiness: A Handbook for Living*, page 52.

17 His Holiness the 14th Dalai Lama and Howard C. Cutler, *The Art of Happiness: A Handbook for Living*, page 13.

Affirmation 18

Purpose

I follow my heart

I pay attention to my feelings

I do the things that make my heart sing

I have the courage

To follow my purpose

I make my own path

18

Purpose

*Do not go where the path may lead,
go instead where there is no path and leave a trail.*
Ralph Waldo Emerson (1803 – 1882)

You were born for a reason.

You were born to experience life, to explore and be who you are - to make a difference. Life is an adventure we undertake. It is a journey.

Following our purpose is like forging your own trail upon the Earth. It means making your own path and not simply following what others do. Your life is your journey. No one before, or after you, will have the same journey. You are unique.

Purpose gives meaning to our lives. It makes us go beyond the everyday. When you are driven by a sense of purpose and meaning, you can tolerate almost anything.

Victor Frankl, a doctor, psychologist and survivor of the Auschwitz concentration camp, wrote about his experiences and his theory that the primary motivation for man is the search for a meaning to life. He stated that it is only through having a sense of purpose and meaning to life that we can survive hardship and suffering and quoted Nietzsche who stated that "He who has a why to live can bear almost any how".[18] Frankl discovered that even in the horrific conditions of the concentration camp, it was the people who had a sense of purpose and meaning and a goal to strive for, who were the most likely to survive. He found that those who had lost a sense of their own future were lost.[19]

Having a sense of purpose and meaning are vital to us. Most of us will never have to endure the devastating conditions of a concentration camp, but even in our lives, if we live without a sense of purpose, our existence may seem like an endless repetition of the same everyday tasks.

Without a sense of purpose, life can seem empty - but everyone has a purpose. No-one's life is empty and meaningless. We all make a difference. Your life and your purpose are unique to you – they are yours alone. There is no right or wrong. What brings meaning to your life is different to what brings meaning to others. What brings meaning to you can, and probably will change, throughout your life. The challenge is to be yourself, to forge your own path along your journey.

You may be driven to do something in particular. This is the feeling at the core of your being that there is something you have to do in life. It is the feeling that something is missing. Until

---

18 Viktor E Frankl, *Man's Search for Meaning,* Pocket Books, New York, 1984, page 97.

Viktor Frankl, a survivor of the Auschwitz concentration camp, writes about his experiences and his theory that the primary motivation for man is the search for a meaning to life. He states that it is only through having a sense of purpose and meaning to life that we can survive hardship and suffering. He quotes Nietzsche who states that "He who has a *why* to live can bear almost any *how*" page 97.

19 Viktor E Frankl, *Man's Search for Meaning*, page 98.

you find out what it is and complete it, your life's experience does not seem complete. For many, their purpose is to simply survive, for some it is to have children, others may be driven to devote their lives for other people. No choice is better or worse than another. There is only what is right for you and only you will know that.

Whatever you are here to do, you will know if you have achieved it by listening to your feelings. Do you feel fulfilled and happy with your life or do you have the feeling deep down that something is missing, that there is something you have left undone?

To find your purpose, follow your heart. What are your true feelings? Where do they lead you? What gives you joy? What would you do if you didn't have to worry about money and had the time and energy to do whatever you want? Your purpose is that which fulfills you.

We all have things we feel we must do that stop us from doing what we want to. But is it really all or nothing? Can you find a way to live your dreams? They are a key to your purpose, a key to your soul – to who you really are.

Life is an opportunity to experience, to grow, to love.

Ultimately, your purpose is to be yourself. To be happy, to love and to be who you are and live in the full expression of who you are. It is then that you will be truly fulfilled.

Affirmation 19

Life is My Mirror

I am conscious of life as my mirror

It is my greatest teacher

I pay attention to what it is showing me

I am a reflection of you

You are a reflection of me

To change the reflection

I need to change me

19

Mirrors

When you meet someone better than yourself,
turn your thoughts to becoming his equal.
When you meet someone not as good as you are,
look within and examine your own self.
Confucius (551 – 479 BC)

We are all connected. Everyone and everything in your life reflects back a facet of you. We are mirrors for each other.

There are many times when you feel that people upset you, make you angry or frustrated. Sometimes we don't like a certain aspect of a person; maybe they are not trustworthy, or they are too loud, too quiet or simply annoying. These are the things that the universe is telling us to pay attention to. Anything that annoys or upsets you does so because it is showing you something about yourself. Any strong reaction that you have to a person or an event, whether the reaction is positive or negative, is not just about the external event or what another person said or did, it is about you.

Everyone that we interact with is a mirror for us. If you are attracting negativity in your life, if something upsets you or makes you angry, it is because it is mirroring something that is in your thoughts, feelings and life.

The universe is providing you with the opportunity to learn more about yourself. You can decide to ignore it, to continue being angry, frustrated or annoyed or you can ask yourself, why am I feeling this way? What is this telling me about myself? Is whatever I am upset about, also something I am doing? It is an opportunity to understand yourself, to move from a state where you are just reacting, to one where you are responding and learning.

Once you look at yourself in this way and deal with the causes, you will no longer attract the same situations. You will be different and therefore you will attract different things into your life.

Thinking of others as a mirror for you clearly shows you where you are at right now. Look at the people around you. What are you attracting in your life? What are the events and people in your life showing you about yourself?

Once you become conscious that your actions, attitude and beliefs are attracting what you have in your life, that people and situations in your life are a mirror for your beliefs, attitudes and thoughts, you can decide if you want to change or not.

Your life is a reflection of everything you think, feel and do. We live in a universe of cause and effect. Looked at in this way, your thoughts, feelings and actions are the cause and your life is the effect. Your life is a mirror of your inner self. If you want to change what is in your life, you need to change your attitude, beliefs and thoughts. Change these and your world will change.

Everyone who touches your life is your teacher if you wish to take the opportunity to learn. We are all connected to each other and a reflection of each other. Your outer world mirrors your inner world. Our world mirrors our collective thoughts, feelings and behaviours. To change any of this, we first need to change ourselves. You need to be the change.

Ultimately, we are all reflections of the universal consciousness of creation.

You are a facet of us. We are facets of you.

Affirmation 20

I Show the Way

I learn, I teach

I show the way

I choose to do this consciously

I will be the love

That will change the world

I create the future

I am the future

20

Show the Way

You must be the change you wish to see in the world.
Mahatma Gandhi (1869 – 1948)

We are all teachers.

We teach and influence others every day whether we are conscious of it or not, just by being ourselves. We teach by example. Our words and our actions impact and influence other people. We are the mirrors for others, as they are the mirror for us.

Your thoughts, decisions and choices are energies that spread through the universe, affecting others and affecting the future of the whole world – creating our world. There is much work to do to bring about a world of peace and love.

We all make a difference. How much of a difference and whether it is a positive one or not for our world is a choice we all make. You don't need to be perfect to teach. Who is perfect on this earth and what does this mean anyway? In most cases we teach what we need to learn. There is so much to learn, to create and to experience. We don't have to wait to know everything before we show others and teach others.

If you want the world to be a different place, then you need to make that change in yourself first. In this way the change you want will radiate as energy from you, affecting others around you, like the ripples on the water expanding outward. You may not know how far your influence will reach, but the fact that you do have an influence is irrefutable.

Being conscious of the influence you have on others enables you to be a more active creator, a more deliberate teacher and influencer. Decide how you want to be and how you want the world to be. Imagine it and live it. Embrace who you are and reclaim your power through conscious choices.

You are a creator and a teacher whether you are aware of it or not.

You show the way.

Affirmation 21

I Am Love

Love empowers me

I accept and love myself

I accept and love others

I create love

I attract love

I am love

21

Love

*Love is the affinity which links and draws together
the elements of the world*
Pierre Teilhard de Chardin (1881 – 1955)

Most of us have heard the saying, "Love makes the world go round." There may be more truth to this saying than we realise. Love is the driving force of creation. Love has no beginning and no end. It just is.

When we think about love we often picture it in our minds as a wonderful, pleasant experience. The blissful view of love is a romantic scene of two people in love walking hand in hand or children and parents enjoying a wonderful time together. This is certainly loving, but it is only a small part of love.

Love is joy but it is also tears. To truly love is selfless. It does not take personal satisfaction into account. It is to totally accept the other person, with no expectation in return. It is to experience the fullness of emotions, of pleasure and pain, to experience good times and difficult times and to still be there.

Loving someone means allowing them to be themselves, to make their own choices, to live their own experiences and to be there for them if they need you. As a parent, loving your child sometimes means protecting them and sometimes it means allowing your child to make their own choices, make mistakes and to work it out for themselves. Love sets you free to be yourself and allows those you love to be themselves.

Love has no expectations. It is not always easy to remove our expectations of the people we love. We sometimes find it easier to give unconditional love to our pets because we have no expectations of them other than they are just there in our lives.

Often we find it easier to love others than to love ourselves. We are often more tolerant of other people's imperfections than we are of our own. To truly love another you need to love yourself, accept yourself and love who you are, without judgement or expectations. Do the things you love. Make time for yourself without feeling guilt. Fill yourself with love and it will be easier to express love.

Love gives us a glimpse of the oneness of all creation. When we love someone or something we feel a connection, a bond, a feeling that we are one with them. Yet we do not lose our individuality.

Love manifests the feeling of being one with each other and still being ourselves. In this way, love is the experience we have here on earth that reflects the spiritual connection we all have.

How can we be one with each other and individual at the same time? I believe that love is the outward demonstration of this reality. Love is oneness, being together and connected whilst still being ourselves. It is a reflection of the unity of creation – how we are one with all of creation and also unique individual beings.

Love helps create the positive connections in our lives. It allows us to accept ourselves and others and helps to dissolve fear.

Love empowers.

Affirmation 22

I Am Powerful

I live in an interconnected web of energy

All possibilities are open to me

My thoughts, feelings and choices create my future

Manifesting possibility into reality

I make a difference

I am powerful

I am the creator of my life

22

You Have the Power

Whether you believe you can do a thing, or not,
You are right.
Henry Ford (1863 – 1947)

At any moment of your life, you have the power to change its direction, to make different choices, to create a new life. There is always an opportunity for change.

You have the power to choose, to create, to be who you want to be. You have the power over your emotions, your feelings and your reactions. You have power over your imagination. The power you have is the power over your own choices, the power over your mind and your thoughts and the power to decide how you will view things. You can decide to change the way you think and this in turn changes the way you feel.

Never underestimate the power of your choices. They literally create your life. All possibilities exist. The universe can be thought of as a web, connecting all of us. Every part is connected to every other part. Some connections we have are very close, others more distant – but the connections are there. The universal web contains all possibilities. All possibilities are open to us. In any given moment our lives can change direction based on the thoughts we have and the choices we make.

We attract possibilities and outcomes to us by our own thoughts, feelings, choices and actions. We all have the power to determine all of those things. We are the power that creates our own lives as we experience it.

Our bodies are like an energy bank. Our energy comes from the three aspects of our being – body, mind and spirit. We deposit or withdraw from our personal energy bank every day. Often we do this without consciously being aware of what we do. All we know is the result – either feeling great or feeling down.

We give or take away energy from our body by what we eat and drink, the exercise we do or don't do, the drugs and chemicals we take or don't take and the way we either love or hate our body.

We give or take away energy from our mind by the things we see and learn – television, games, learning, reading, experiencing something new - things that either stimulate our minds or let them stagnate.

We give or take away energy from our soul or spirit by the way we feel and act towards ourselves and other people.

All three aspects are interrelated – in fact they are three aspects of the one being. How we feel about ourselves and others affects how we think and how we act. If we want to change something about our lives, gain personal energy and empower ourselves, we need to work on how we feel.

Inner strength and personal power does not mean having power over another person. To be empowered means to have the personal strength to accept that you are responsible for your life and will decide how you are going to respond to things that happen to you. It is to take responsibility for your thoughts, actions and choices. It is to be conscious that you create your life.

You are in control and have the power to change the outcome and direction of your life if you choose. You may not always be able to control what happens to you but you can always control how you respond to what happens. Blaming others for your choices is choosing powerlessness. It is feeling that you are at the mercy of something or someone else, that you are not in control of your life and your reactions. It is like drifting in the sea – allowing other forces to direct you.

Your energy is your personal power and it is primarily about the way you feel. Everything else follows. No-one can control the way you feel.

Think about life in these terms – the universe is like a connected web and all possibilities are open to you. Your choices attract the circumstances of your life. They also affect the circumstances of others. You make a difference. Your existence, your thoughts and choices not only affect you, but act on those around you.

You have the power to create your life and to change the direction of your life if you wish. Empower yourself to be the person you want to be.

Realise how powerful you are.

Affirmation 23

I Make a Difference

I make a difference

My very existence has changed the world

I have choices to make

Consciously or unconsciously

My choices will affect me and everyone around me

I am conscious of the difference I make

I realise how powerful I am

23

You Make a Difference

*People travel to wonder at the height of the mountains,
at the huge waves of the seas, at the long course of the rivers,
at the vast compass of the ocean, at the circular motion of the stars,
and yet they pass by themselves without wondering.*
St. Augustine (354 – 430 AD)

You make a difference. You affect the future of the world. Through your very existence you have changed and will change the future.

It is easy to feel small sometimes - a small being on a small planet that is part of an enormously vast universe, yet remember there is no one else like you; there never was and there never will be. You are unique. Love that about yourself.

We often take ourselves for granted. Seeing the wonder of nature and our Earth but forgetting that we are part of that nature. We are amazing creatures with an incredible inventive power and the ability to change our world.

We often take our Earth for granted. We marvel at the other planets, at a crater on Mars or the rings around Saturn. These are indeed marvellous, but we forget the incredible beauty and features of our own Earth, which has given birth to the mountains, oceans, land, plants and animals, including us.

You are more than one in a million. Have you ever thought about the incredible sequence of events that had to occur for you to exist? If your parents hadn't met, or your grandparents or great grandparents, then you would not exist. If you hadn't been conceived at the exact moment you were, then you wouldn't exist.

Realise how incredible it is that you have the wonderful gift of life. Is it chance that you were born? Maybe, maybe not. Either way, you have the gift of life - the certainty of making a difference in the world. The world would be a different place if you did not exist.

Think about the people whose lives you affect. You come into contact with people every day and that contact may change their life and change your life. Every thought you have, every choice you make affects you and the people around you.

Every day, every decision, action or inaction you make has consequences that affect your life and the lives of others. Some may have only a minor effect; other choices have major consequences for you and others. Each choice sets up a ripple effect of consequences – one leading to another that affects not just you, but everyone around you. We never know how far our influence stretches.

We don't always know the full impact of our actions. We are aware of some, but our decisions, actions and words may have a more far reaching impact than we can imagine. Even the smallest actions can make a difference – either positively or negatively. When you smile at someone on the street, give a beggar some money or help someone in only a small way, you don't know the impact you may have. Equally, an angry word or ridicule may have far greater consequences than you realise.

I think about the person who pulled me back from being hit by a car. I don't know who he was but he saved my life. He might not even remember the incident. It was before I had children. In a very real sense, even my children owe their life to the actions of this man.

Your existence on Earth means that you make a difference. How much of a difference and what kind of a difference is up to you.

Affirmation 24

The World is in My Hands

I am a creator

I am connected to everything else

My thoughts, feelings and actions matter

What affects me affects everything

To change the world, I need to change myself

The world is in my hands

24

Our World

A human being is a part of the whole called by us universe, a part limited in time and space. He experiences himself, his thoughts and feeling as something separated from the rest, a kind of optical delusion of his consciousness. This delusion is a kind of prison for us, restricting us to our personal desires and to affection for a few persons nearest to us. Our task must be to free ourselves from this prison by widening our circle of compassion to embrace all living creatures and the whole of nature in its beauty.
Albert Einstein (1879 – 1955)

Imagine a world where we all live consciously, aware that our actions, our thoughts and our feelings create our lives and our future.

Imagine a world where we are all consciously choosing and taking responsibility for our choices. Imagine a world where we acknowledge, live and act, knowing that we are all connected to each other and one with everything in existence.

Imagine a world where we treat each other the way we want to be treated ourselves.

Imagine a world where we recognise that each of us is really a part of one interconnected whole - one universal energy consciousness.

Imagine a world of peace, love, trust and respect for all – all life, the earth and the world. Imagine this world and how it would be.

You can create this world. It starts with each one of us.

This world may seem to be impossible to create. Our reality at present seems so far away from this. On a global scale, there are wars, famine and terrorism. Closer to home there is violence, racism, crime and indifference to the plight of others. Fear abounds and that fear creates the environment for all of this negativity.

It is fear that leads one group to fight another – fear of being overtaken, fear of losing their identity, fear that they will no longer be superior, fear of losing control, fear that if they give to others, they will have less themselves, fear that people will harm them so they better get in first. Fear leads to anger – that others have more than they do, anger that things seem unjust – that they are disadvantaged compared to other groups. Anger leads to retaliation and all of this has its basis in fear. Fear has its basis in the idea that we are separate from one another – that we will be disadvantaged unless we strike first.

The reality is that no-one has to lose for us to win. There is enough for everyone if we only change our thinking. Giving to others does not mean we lose. Letting others be free does not mean we will lose our freedom. Like attracts like. When our thinking is one of fear, of lack, that is what we attract to us. There is no separation in our universe. If we are free in our giving, free in our thinking that the universe will provide whatever we need, then we will attract what we need and want. It is not a competition. Striking against others affects us too.

The opposite of fear is love. Love is inclusive and all encompassing and there is a great deal of love in the world. We have all witnessed the outpouring of assistance given to people around the world who have suffered as a result of natural disasters – the differences between us vanish. We no longer see race, religion, poor or rich – we see humanity, we see ourselves and we are moved to help. Is it too far-fetched to imagine a world where we help each other at all times and work to help those in need?

If we want a world of peace and love, then we need to be and do that first ourselves. The only things we can control are our own thoughts and actions. If we want a world where we all live consciously and take responsibility for our actions, then we first need to do these ourselves.

Life is a process of creation and it is our creation. Each one of us creates our reality and cumulatively, we all create the events and circumstances of the world.

There are infinite possibilities that can be created in any moment and we draw and attract to us a particular possibility through our thoughts and through our decisions and choices. What we sometimes don't realise is how powerful our choices, actions and reactions are.

We are one with each other. We are creators. What we create is up to each of us. What you create is up to you.

We all hold the world in the palms of our hands.

Affirmation 25

I Am Infinity

There is no end

Only stages along my journey

Past, present, future

It is all now

I am the Creator

I am one with everything

I AM

25

Infinity

To see a World in a Grain of Sand
And a Heaven in a Wild Flower,
Hold Infinity in the palm of your hand
And Eternity in an hour.
William Blake (1757-1827), Auguries of Innocence

I end this book with a reflection poem on Infinity. We are energy and consciousness. Energy does not die; it changes form but continues to exist. Perhaps in the same way, there is no end for us - there is only the eternal journey.

At the end

There is no end

Only stages

Along the journey

It is an eternal

Search for home

Although home is where

You have always been

There is no right

There is no wrong

There is only experience

And growth

There is change

There is stillness

Past, present, future

It is all now

We are unique

We are the same

We are an expression

Of the creator's thoughts

Yet we are the creator

Time and eternity

There is no end

We are one

You are

I AM

Infinity

About the Author

Antoinette Pellegrini

It's not easy to write about yourself and try to describe who you are in a few sentences but I hope this tells you a little about me and my journey so far.

I live in a leafy Melbourne suburb in Victoria, Australia. I am a Mind Body Medicine practitioner, Holistic Counsellor,

Mindfulness Coach and Reiki Master practitioner and teacher. I am also a qualified secondary school teacher and worked as a teacher for a number of years before beginning a corporate career.

Life hasn't always been easy. There have been health issues to contend with and relationship breakups, the most significant of which was the end of my marriage when my eldest son was two years old and my youngest only three months old. I was still on maternity leave from work when my husband left. To say that it was a difficult time is an understatement. Bringing up two boys as a single mother is not easy. I chose to go back to a corporate job when my youngest was six months old as I believed that this would allow me to provide for my sons and give them a good education. Now my sons are adults and are wonderful and caring men.

I still wonder whether going back to a corporate job was the right decision. I wonder what would have happened if I had stayed home with them, allowing me more time with them but also allowing me more time for me to fulfil my own dreams and passions. I will never know but regardless, it was the decision that brought me to where I am today.

What I have written about in this book are the things that I have struggled with all my life.

I was an atheist, believing that God, or something beyond this life, did not exist. I now believe and have experienced first-hand that there is something beyond this life and it is within our power to experience this now if we are open to it.

My intuition has always been strong but at key times of my life, I did not listen. I have taken many difficult paths because of this – paths that I knew about if only I had paid attention to my own feelings.

I have struggled with anger, fear and blaming others for the outcomes of my life, which left me feeling powerless with little, if any, self-confidence. I now live my life knowing that I create my life and that I have total control over how I react to what occurs in life. I know being positive draws positivity into my life. I know that I am the creator of my life and that I change the possibilities into my reality by what I am thinking, feeling and how I act and react. This has made me feel happier, stronger and more empowered. My goals are becoming easier to manifest.

I have been in relationships where I have totally lost my identity in the hope of holding on to someone's love. I now know that the only way to really be whole in a relationship is to be true to who I am.

I have spent most of my early years so caught up with the past or worrying about possible future events that I have not enjoyed the only thing I had – the present moment. I am now learning and practising to be more mindful and am helping others to appreciate and be grateful for their lives.

I am now at the point in my life when, being able to leave the corporate job, I have begun to work and live the life that enables me to fulfil what I now see as my life's purpose. Writing this book has been an important step in this process.

I am looking forward to the rest of my journey.

The Thought Connection

Mindfulness, Wellbeing and Conscious Living

Antoinette Pellegrini is the Owner and Manager of The Thought Connection.

The mind plays an important part in overall health and wellbeing. The mission for The Thought Connection is to help empower people to realise their potential for health and happiness and overall wellbeing of body, mind and spirit.

A key aspect of this is to help people realise that they are in control of their lives and that their thinking affects their health, wellbeing and literally creates their future. This represents the thought connection – the connection that thinking plays in all aspects of life.

The aim is to work from a holistic perspective to assist with the management of pain and stress, shift negative thought and behaviour patterns, help improve overall health, wellbeing and happiness and to help people achieve their goals.

One on one consultations are tailored to the individual and include a combination of natural healing modalities, holistic counselling and mindfulness techniques. Antoinette also runs workshops on personal development, mindfulness, and meditation.

Website: www.thethoughtconnection.com

Table of Contents

- ANTI-INFLAMMATORY DIET: 2 IN 1 BUNDLE 1
- 100% PALEO: 1
- ALKALINE PALEO MIX & PALEO DIET FOR WEIGHT LOSS AND HEALTH 1
- BY ELENA GARCIA AND JAMES ADLER 1
- TABLE OF CONTENTS 3

BOOK 1 1

- INTRODUCTION 2
  - WHO ARE WE AND WHY WE WROTE THIS BOOK 2
- FREE COMPLIMENTARY EBOOK + NEWSLETTER 5
- CHAPTER 1: ALKALIZE WITH AN ANCIENT TWIST 6
  - ALKALINE: ELENA'S STRONG POINT 6
  - ALKALINE VS. ACIDIC? 8
  - BEFORE WE DIVE INTO COMPLICATED PH DISCUSSIONS, HERE IS ONE THING TO UNDERSTAND: 8
- CHAPTER 2 ALKALINE PALEO BREAKFASTS TO START YOUR DAY WITH A BANG 25
  - RECIPE #1 ALKALINITY SCRAMBLE 26
  - RECIPE#2 BELLY BREAKFAST 28
  - RECIPE#3 SALMON-Y SLIDERS 31
  - RECIPE#4 PALEO-PACKED PEPPERS 33
  - RECIPE#5 APPLE-SAUSAGE SQUASH SALAD 34
  - RECIPE#6 BREAKFAST BAKE 35
  - RECIPE#7 SPICY SWEET POTATOES 36
  - RECIPE#8 BERRY BEEFY 37
  - RECIPE #8 YUMMY SHRIMP VEGGIE STIR-FRY 38
  - RECIPE#9 SIMPLE OREGANO TUNA STIR FRY 39
  - RECIPE#10 VEGAN PALEO BREAKFAST 41
- CHAPTER 3: LASTING LUNCHES: ALKALINE WITH A SPLASH OF PALEO 42
  - RECIPE#11 SALMON SALAD SANDWICHES WITH SIMPLE SALAD ON THE SIDE 43
  - RECIPE#12 SWEET POTATO BREAD 44
  - RECIPE#13 SIMPLE SALAD 45
  - RECIPE#14 CARNE ASADA WITH KALE CHIPS N' SPINACH GUACAMOLE 46

- Recipe#15 Guac 48
- Recipe#16 Kale Chips 49
- Recipe#17 Soup n' Souper-Salad 50
- Recipe#18 Soup 52
- Recipe#19 Chicken-Strip Salad 53
- Recipe#20 Salad 54
- Recipe#21 Asian Meatballs with Noodles 55
- Recipe#22 Simple Vegan Paleo Salad 57

CHAPTER 4 DELECTABLE ALKALINE DINNERS 58

- Recipe#23 Bison Balls and Roast Veggies 59
- Recipe#24 Roast Veggies 60
- Recipe#25 Barbeque Chicken and Coleslaw 61
- Recipe#26 Coleslaw 62
- Recipe#27 Italian Beef 63
- Recipe#28 Zucchini Noodles 65
- Recipe#29 Topped Tilapia with Kale Salad 66
- Recipe#30 Krispy Kale Salad 67
- Recipe#31 Chicken, Sprouts, n Spuds 68
- Recipe#32 Spuds 69

BONUS CHAPTER: ALKALINE PALEO SALADS 70

- Recipe#32 Apple and Celery Root Salad 71
- Recipe#33 Samphire Roast Lemon and Hazelnut Salad 72
- Recipe#34 Green Papaya Salad 74
- Recipe#35 Summer Slaw with Tahini Coconut Dressing 75
- Recipe#36 Raw Broccoli Slaw 77

FREE COMPLIMENTARY EBOOK 79

CONCLUSION: TAKE POSITIVE ACTION TODAY! 80

BOOK 2 81

PALEO DIET FOR WEIGHT LOSS AND HEALTH 81

GET BACK TO YOUR PALEOLITHIC ROOTS, LOSE MASSIVE WEIGHT AND BECOME A SEXY PALEO CAVEMAN/ CAVEWOMAN!!! 81

WWW.HOLISTICWELLNESSBOOKS.COM .... ERROR! BOOKMARK NOT DEFINED.

- My Paleo Experience 83

DO YOU WANT TO JOIN ME? 83

FREE COMPLIMENTARY EBOOK 86

CHAPTER 1 PALEO LIFESTYLE MADE EASY 87

CHAPTER 2 LOSING WEIGHT WITH PALEO 92

CHAPTER 3 HOW TO GET STARTED? 97

CHAPTER 4 BASIC PALEO RECIPES FOR WEIGHT LOSS AND VITALITY 104

BREAKFAST 106

    #1. PAN-CAVES 107

    #2. EASY PALEO SCRAMBLE 108

    #3. SPINACH AND BRUSSELS FRITTATA 109

LUNCH 110

    #4. SPICY TUNA WITH ARTICHOKES 111

    #6. MEXICAN CHICKEN SALAD 113

DINNER 114

    #7. ZUCCHINI CHICKEN 115

    #8. BACON-TOPPED MEATLOAF 116

    #9 SAUTÉED KALE 117

    #10. ONE DISH FISH 118

CHAPTER 5 PALEO HEALTHY SNACKS: HOW TO AVOID CHEATING? 119

    #12 PALEO YUMMY CAKE 123

    #13 VEGGIES INNA CAVE 124

    #14 ALKALINE PALEO MIX 126

    #15 SALMON ROCKS! 127

    #16 PALEO BACON BRUSSELS SPROUTS WITH TWIST 128

    #17 MINI RECIPE: GUACAMOLE AND BACON 130

    #18. CREAMY BOLOGNESE SAUCE 131

    #19. CLASSIC PALEO BREAKFAST 133

    #20. JAMAICAN PALEOLITHIC TWIST 134

THIS IS A REALLY NICE, SPICY, TROPICAL PALEO FRIENDLY MEAL. GREAT FOR DINNERS WITH FRIENDS! 134

    #21. CHERRY BERRY PALEO DELIGHT 136

    #24. SHRIMP STUFFED AVOCADOS 137

I LOVE THIS RECIPE AS A HEALTHY SNACK. 137

PREPARATION: 137

    #25. Paleolized Chicken and Vegetable Soup 138

    #26. BEET SOUP AND ALGA DULSE 140

    #27. AVOCADO SALAD WITH SEA SPAGHETTI ALGA 141

    #28. Apple Paleo Agar Agar Dream Dessert (no sugar or fructose) 142

    #29. Seaweed Salad and Avocado. 143

    #30. Kiwi Wakame Paleo Smoothie. 144

    #31. Japanese Paleo Twist. 146

    #32 Weight Loss Paleo Apple Pudding 147

    #33. Paleo Hiziki Time. 148

    #34. Paleo Seewood Spaghetti 149

PREPARATION: 149

    #35. Wakame seaweed salad 150

    #36. Paleo Sardinas Like whisky! 151

    #37. Easy Seaweed Salad 152

PREPARATION: 152

    #38. Fishy Paleolithic Taste 153

PREPARATION: 153

    #39. Paleo Tuna with Algae 154

    #40. Sexy Skinny 155

CHAPTER 7 PALEO MOTIVATION FOR LIFETIME 156

FREE COMPLIMENTARY EBOOK 165

Book 1

Alkaline Paleo Mix: How to Combine Paleo Diet and Alkaline Diet for Wellness, Weight Loss, and Vibrant Health

By Elena Garcia and James Adler

**Copyright Elena Garcia and James Adler©
2014, 2016**

Introduction

Would you like to improve your overall health, detox your body on a daily basis, experience endless amounts of energy, lose weight, rev up your sex drive, and boost your mental capacity? Sure, we all would. Yet, most people do not know that you can have all of this simply by changing what you eat.

The good news is that with this book, you will be able to prepare interesting delicious, mouthwatering meals to revolutionize your health and life. When it comes to "dieting", it's not only about weight loss. It's about deep personal transformation and realizing how much you can actually achieve if you get committed to it.

No longer will you have to look for the newest energy drink, supplement, pill, or workout plan that will bring health and wellness. Your search stops here. Slow the process of aging, rid yourself of digestive issues and allergies, and feel better than you ever have before! At the same time, we would like to let you know that there will be no starvation involved. We propose a healthy and balanced diet that is also delicious and will satisfy your taste buds.

WHO ARE WE AND WHY WE WROTE THIS BOOK

We are Elena(Ela) and James, a married couple who found out that through the combination of two of the best dietary plans (we were each a fan of different ones), the marriage of Paleo and Alkaline, we could have everything we have ever wanted or needed in order to mentally and physically function at our finest!! We wanted to share our combined efforts with everyone, which is why we put together this book. There is both a female as well as a male point of view.

Introduction

We have outlined the basics of our combined efforts, providing you with an easy to understand breakdown of Alkaline Paleo nutrition. Included are shopping lists and recipes that will not only provide you with delicious meals, they will inevitably change your life forever! Put together these meals and provide your body and mind with what they need to allow you to successfully live a healthy, energized lifestyle today. It's easy, fun and exciting. There is no need to survive entirely on greens, we are fans of balance and this is what we want to teach you.

The book you are reading now is our practical vision of how you can combine Alkaline-Paleo diets and create something that works for you. In order to be successful, you should be enjoying your process of transformation. We encourage you to do what we did- experiment and come up with your plan that is exciting and full of nutrients. This book is not strictly Alkaline, we believe that it's all about balance. We have seen way too many of our friends fail with their wellness and weight loss goals because they were trying to be perfect and thought that it was all about eating 100% green alkaline foods. This may be a good idea for an occasional detox plan conducted with an experienced nutritionist, but we personally do not recommended it as an everyday eating plan. We try to be as transparent as possible and simply tell you what we do. Take what you like and reject the rest. We encourage you to take notes as you read, in case you have any questions, suggestions and doubts, simply email us at:

elenajamesbooks@gmail.com

Our mission is to make things as easy and simple as possible-no fluff. There is no need to devour dozens of advanced nutrition books to be healthy. If you are a busy parent, like we both are, we understand that it can be pretty challenging to eat healthy and keep it tasty at the same time. This is why we came up with an idea of writing a practical dieting book that is full of tips and recipes that you can implement straight away and see results. We suggest you start applying as soon as possible- you will be blown away by the results. Healthy eating is actually easy and fun!

Introduction

We wish you weight loss and health success, thanks again for taking interest in our little book, we really do hope you and your family will find it helpful!

Introduction

Free Complimentary eBook + Newsletter

Interested in health, wellness and healthy eating? Join our Alkaline Paleo newsletter to be the first one to be notified about our new releases at a discounted price (+ giveaways, wellness news + much much more!).

As a welcome gift, you will receive a free copy of our book Alkaline Paleo Superfoods!

Download link:

www.holisticwellnessbooks.com/bonus

Problems with your download?

Contact us: elenajamesbooks@gmail.com

We will make sure you receive your free eBook as promised.

Chapter 1: Alkalize with an Ancient Twist

By combining two strange sounding, different nutritional lifestyles, we were able to come up with a single dietary plan that is the perfect fit for two equally different and strange people! If it works for us, it can work for you. The key is in the fact that both of these lifestyles were created to help the body function the way that it was designed to. They are set up in a manner that allows them to work *with* the body, instead of fighting to keep it inline. Mixing these blueprint-like nutritional guidelines will allow you to be in spectacular physical and mental health for the rest of your life!

Alkaline: Elena's strong point

The object of eating an alkaline diet is not what it sounds like it might be. There is no battery-eating involved. The objective is to alkalize your body by eating foods and drinking liquids that will encourage a balanced pH environment. The blood's pH is designed to run effectively at 7.35 A "normal," modern diet is full of foods and substances that, when digested, have an acidic effect on the system, causing many problems. Many unwanted health issues can be related to:

- Heart disease
- Allergies
- Gastro-intestinal issues
- Chronic inflammation
- Respiratory problems
- Obesity
- Arthritis

Chapter 1: Alkalize with an Ancient Twist

- Skin ailments
- Immune system function
- Hair Loss
- Sexual Dysfunctions
- Muscular, reproductive, excretory, and nervous system malfunctions

In order to get your pH back on track and in balance, it is recommended that we focus on eating 70- 80 percent alkaline forming food. The other 20-30 percent is allowed to be acid-forming (where we decided to apply our "Paleo meat," more on that later). The acid-forming foods should be of course as healthy as possible, I suggest you avoid/eliminate processed foods. The alkaline foods you will need to focus on are mainly vegetables; some non-sugary fruits are allowable (you can keep all kinds of fruits in your acidic 20-30% of your diet).

This was actually easy for me to do (Elena). I enjoyed a vegan diet for most of my adult life and already had a taste for high alkaline foods. Hydration is also a big part of alkalizing the body and I would normally drink so much water that it would make some people balk. James always thought one day I would float away! The first thing I do in the morning is…I .drink a few glasses of alkaline water and I add some green powders. I also like to squeeze in some fresh lemon juice. I usually drink about 1 liter of good quality alkaline water first thing in the morning. It's excellent for digestion!

I believe that alkaline supplements are also extremely important; however the first thing you should focus on is consuming more fresh, alkaline foods. Supplements won't do miracles if you still cheat and stick to your old, unhealthy habits.

Generally we stick to green and root veggies, some fruits, and seeds/nuts. While animal meats and eggs make up most of the other 30-20%. We all do green juice fast about once or twice a year. We also do at least one raw food weekend a month. This is when we give our bodies and digestive tracks some really well-deserved rest. James finds it hard as he loves his meat. But after each cleanse he feels so good that he is utterly grateful I convinced him to join me in this amazing process of detoxification.

Alkaline vs. Acidic?

Sounds like the title fight for a light weight boxing match. In reality it is a fight, a fight for the pH balance of your body. pH levels are basically the measure of how acidic a liquid is. Our bodies function optimally when our blood is at about 7.35 ph. which is slightly alkaline.

Before we dive into complicated pH discussions, here is one thing to understand:

-The alkaline <u>diet is not about changing or "raising" your pH</u>. This is where many alkaline guides go wrong. You see, our body is smart enough to self-regulate our pH for us. Unfortunately, when you constantly bombard your body with acid-forming foods (for example processed foods, fast food, alcohol, sugar, and even too much meat) you torture your body with an incredible stress. Why? Well because it has to work harder to maintain that optimal pH…

Here's simple example…

Imagine you immerse yourself in a bath filled with ice. You say, but hey, my body can self-regulate its optimal temperature, right? And yes, it can. But it will eventually collapse and you will get ill. The same happens with nutrition and our blood's pH. You can spend years indulging in toxic, processed, acid-forming foods that only deprive your body of its vital nutrients, saying: "But hey, my body will self-regulate its optimal blood pH".

And again, it will...but sooner or later it will give up and manifest a disease. It will accumulate fat as its natural defense function to protect your body from over-acidity. We don't wanna end up there, right?

So, to sum up- the alkaline diet is a natural, holistic system, a nutritional lifestyle that advocates consumption of fresh, unprocessed foods that are rich in nutrients. These are called alkaline foods and they help your body stimulate its optimal healing functions. Yes! A healthy body needs nutrients and fresh fruits and vegetables are great for that.

The problem is that nowadays, most diets are filled with acid-forming foods that eventually make it hard for the body to regulate its optimal, healthy blood pH and artificial sweeteners do the same. Acidosis is very common in this day and age thanks to things we drink as well: coffee, alcohol, and sodas all have an acidic effect on our bodies. Not to mention the chemicals many people take in through things like smoking and drugs (even prescription drugs have this effect).

There are many ways that you could become acidic. Eating acid forming foods, stress, taking in too many toxins, and bodily processes all cause acidity in the body. Our internal systems try to balance themselves out and bring pH up with the help of alkaline minerals that we can ingest through our diet. If we do not take in a higher percentage of alkaline than acidic foods, we can become too acidic.

When you are acidic, it makes every process that your body normally does much more difficult or impossible for it to accomplish. We cannot absorb the beneficial nutrients we need from our food properly. Our cells are not able to produce energy efficiently. Our bodies are not able to fix damaged cells properly. We will not be able to detoxify properly. Fatigue and illness will drag you down.

Changing your diet to one that is full of alkaline foods is one of the easiest and best things you can do for your overall health. We were so ecstatic that we did! If you are acidic, as we were, you should change your diet immediately. You should aim to intake 70-80 percent alkaline-forming foods. Sounds pretty easy, right?

What are alkaline foods? Is it about their pH?

No, luckily it's much, much easier. We don't care about the food's pH in its natural form...All we care about is the effect that the food has on the body after it has been consumed and metabolized. For example, lemons, grapefruits and limes are considered alkaline-forming foods.

What? Elena? James! Are you out of your mind? Everyone knows lemons are acidic...

Well, let us repeat again. Lemons are acidic as far as their taste and ph. in their natural state are concerned. But, they are full of alkaline minerals and low in sugar which makes them alkaline-forming foods.

At the same time, oranges contain more sugar which makes them less alkaline-forming.

Let us repeat:

Some charts determine acidity or alkalinity of the food before it is consumed & others (like the ones we follow and recommend) are more interested in the effect the food has on the body after it has been consumed.

It's really that simple!

As a general rule, alkaline foods are:
-rich in minerals and vitamins
-fresh, not packaged
-not fermented
-low in sugar (all kinds of sugar are acid-forming)
-plant-based
-mostly raw or slightly cooked
-caffeine-free
-chemical-free
-provide hydration
-naturally gluten-free

So let's have a look at the food lists. We think that after our intro it will be easier for you to understand the difference between alkaline and acid forming foods, even without looking at the charts...

One more thing- we base our food lists on Doctor Young's latest research.

We know it is quite confusing to see so many different charts online. We have been there.

The reason why so many other charts show such disparity is because they base their classifications on the readings for the so called PRAL which stands for Potential Renal Acid Load research. Unfortunately, this is not a reliable source of practical information for us.

Why?

Well PRAL tests burn the food at an extreme temperature and then take a read of the 'ash' that is left behind and what it's pH is.

While this will give a read of its alkalinity from the mineral content of the food, by burning it at such a high temperature they also burn away sugar. And sugar is very acid-forming...

That is why on some charts high sugar fruits are listed as super alkaline. Now we are not saying that fruits are bad for you, most fruits are neutral or mildly alkaline forming and great as a natural snack or a part of a balanced diet. But they are not as alkalizing as most veggies are.

Some charts determine acidity or alkalinity on the food before it is consumed & others like the ones we list below, are more interested in the effect the food has on the body after it has been consumed.

ALKALIZING VEGETABLES

Asparagus
Broccoli
Chili
Pepper
Zucchini
Dandelion
Snowpeas
Green Beans
String Beans
Runner Beans
Spinach
Kale
Wakame
Kelp
Collards
Chives
Endive
Chard
Cabbage
Sweet Potato
Mint
Ginger
Coriander
Basil
Brussels Sprouts
Cauliflower
Carrot

Beetroot
Eggplant
Garlic
Onion
Parsley
Celery
Cucumber
Watercress
Lettuce
Peas
Broad Beans
New Potato
Pumpkin
Radish

ALKALIZING FRUITS
Avocado
Tomato
Lemon
Lime
Grapefruit
Fresh Coconut
Pomegranate

ALKALIZING PROTEIN
Almonds,
Chestnuts,
Protein Powders (we love hemp)

ALKALINE OILS
Avocado Oil
Coconut Oil
Flax Oil
Udo's Oil
Olive Oil

Other:
Alkaline Water

Fresh Almond Milk
Herbal Tea

ALKALINE SUPERFOODS:
Wheatgrass
Barley Grass
Kamut Grass
Dog Grass
Shave Grass
Oat Grass
Soy Sprouts
Alfalfa Sprouts
Amaranth Sprouts
Broccoli Sprouts

ALKALIZING SWEETENERS
-Stevia (natural)

ALKALIZING SPICES & SEASONINGS
-Chili Peppers,
-Cinnamon,
-Curry,
-Ginger,
-Herbs,
-Sea Salt,

ALKALIZING NUTS AND SEEDS
Almonds
Coconut
Flax Seeds
Pumpkin Seeds
Sesame Seeds
Sunflower Seeds

ACID SWEETENERS
Carob, Corn Syrup, Sugar

ACID BEVERAGES

Alcohol, Coffee, Soda

ACID TOXINS AND DRUGS
All drugs, Weed killers, Insecticides, Tobacco

ACID MEAT:
Bacon
Beef
Clams
Corned Beef
Eggs
Lamb
Lobster
Mussels
Organ Meats
Venison
Fish
Oyster
Pork
Rabbit
Sausage
Scallops
Shellfish
Shrimp
Tuna
Turkey
Veal

MIDLY ACID-FORMING/NEUTRAL FRUITS:
Apple
Apricot
Currants
Dates
Grapes
Mango
Peach
Pear
Prunes

Raisins
Raspberries
Strawberries
Tropical Fruits
Cantaloupe
Cranberries
Currants
Honeydew Melon
Orange
Pineapple
Plum

ACID FORMING DAIRY AND EGGS
Butter
Cheese
Milk
Whey
Yogurt
Cottage Cheese
Ice Cream
Sour Cream
Soy Cheese
Eggs

ACID FORMING OILS
Cooked Oil
Solid Oil (Margarine)
Oil Exposed to Heat,
Light or Air

ACID FORMING DRINKS
Alcohol
Black Tea
Coffee
Carbonated Water
Pasteurized Juice
Cocoa

Chapter 1: Alkalize with an Ancient Twist

Energy Drinks
Sports Drinks
Colas
Tap Water
Milk
Green Tea
Decaffeinated Drinks
Flavoured Water

ACID-FORMING SAUCES
Mayonnaise
Ketchup
Mustard
Soy Sauce
Pickles
Vinegar
Tabasco
Tamari
Wasabi

Other ACID-FORMING FOODS:
Mushrooms
Miso
White Breads, Pastas,
Rice & Noodles
Chocolate
Chips
Pizza
Biscuits
Cigarettes
Drugs
Candy!

Use charts as a guide, but don't worry too much if you find it difficult to memorize or if you have doubts whether your favorite food is alkaline

Chapter 1: Alkalize with an Ancient Twist

enough. I, Elena, keep one of my 'alkaline charts' in my wallet at all times to reference at the grocery store!

FREE DOWNLOAD COMPLIMENTARY

We also have easy printable charts that you can download at no cost-

www.holisticwellnessbooks.com/charts

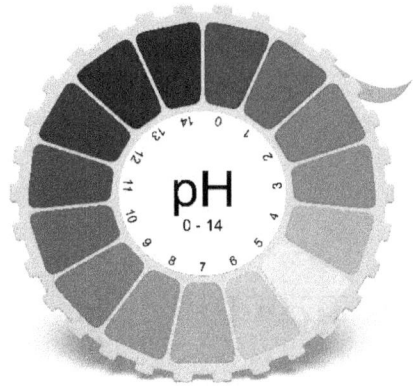

Problems with your download?
Email us at: elenajamesbooks@gmail.com

Also remember to get: http://www.holisticwellnessbooks.com/bonus

Now, that being said, or *read* rather, here are some ways to really boost the alkalinity of your diet!

1. <u>Root vegetables are awesome!</u>
   They are known for their healing power, you will find them used extensively in Chinese medicinal practices. They are also high in their mineral count. Turnip, beet, carrot, and rutabaga are all

Chapter 1: Alkalize with an Ancient Twist

great examples of yummy alkaline root vegetables that will make your mouth water and are easily integrated into a variety of recipes (creative salads and soups).

2. <u>The cruciferous variety will really enhance your alkalinity and your menu!</u>
They are full of vitamins and minerals. They add fiber and are downright tasty. Don't limit yourself to broccoli or cauliflower; forget not the cabbage or Brussels sprouts because they will add a unique flavor to many dishes. These are great steamed and then blended into creamy soups. We love to spice up our alkaline soups with a bit of chicken or fish. This is how we create our alkaline paleo mix and stick to the balanced alkaline rule of 70/30 (or even better 80/20- more on that at the end of this chapter).

3. <u>Do not leave out the leaves!</u>
Leafy green vegetables are super alkalizing and can be added to or based around many recipes. Spinach, a variety of kale, Swiss chard, are my top three and are included in most of the meals that I eat in some way, shape or form. They are brimming with alkalizing essentials. Get committed to green, alkaline smoothies. If you can't stand the taste, or even the mere thought of having a green smoothie, simply blend in a banana, some coconut milk, cinnamon and nutmeg- so yummy and healthy, even kale can taste awesome, right?).

4. <u>Garlic is miraculous.</u>
It is a detoxifying agent and is on many different health food lists. It will work as an antibiotic as well as being antifungal. It lowers blood-pressure and is a serious disease killer. Let us not forget how it easily adds flavor to an innumerable amount of dishes. Of course, nobody wants to overdose garlic (I guess we don't need to explain why?). We recommend you add half of a small garlic clove (minced) to your salad. It will make it taste delicious and help you detoxify, yet you won't experience bad breath. You can also mix ¼-1/2 garlic clove with your veggie smoothies and juices to give it more taste. We also go as far as

Chapter 1: Alkalize with an Ancient Twist

using cumin and curry in our smoothies. We very often convert them into creamy soups. We just can't recommend coconut and almond milk enough. Both alkaline and paleo friendly!

5. <u>Cayenne pepper will add spice to your alkaline life.</u>
   Capsicum is a super spice for alkalinity. It also works as an antibacterial agent in your system. Many people do not know that it contains vitamin A. You can add cayenne to many recipes (soups, juices, salads) or just drink mixed with water. We like to mix cayenne pepper with some olive oil and create our amazingly spicy dressing for salads. We also throw in some herbs like rosemary and thyme. These are both alkaline and paleo friendly.

6. <u>Limes and lemons are a great way to up the alkaline ante!</u>
   They may seem acidic at first, because they taste acidic, but when they are processed by the body, they have an alkaline forming effect- this is what determines their alkalinity. They will stimulate your liver aiding in detoxification. They contain large amounts of vitamin C as well. Squeeze them into your water and add them to a variety of meals! Don't forget to serve your salads and other meals like veggie stirs with a slice of lemon or a small glass of fresh lemon or lime juice. Grapefruits are also extremely alkaline. Oranges are more acidic but still healthy. If you want to have an orange juice, make sure you use fresh, organic lemons and mix it with a bit of alkaline water. High content of Vitamin C makes oranges alkaline, unfortunately they are also rich in sugars which makes them acidic. We love oranges and so do our kids, and we use them as a healthy treat. However, we have gotten used to lemons and grapefruits and we use these to detoxify and reach a healthy, alkaline balance in our lives.

<u>Paleo</u>: James' favorite part

Paleo is just my way of life and I have been following a balanced Paleo lifestyle (at least 90% Paleo) for more than 5 years now. Whenever asked if switching to Paleo was easy, I must admit that it wasn't. But the

Chapter 1: Alkalize with an Ancient Twist

moment I began to see results, I fell in love with Paleo and it became my second nature. I really do believe that this diet was designed for carnivorous animals, like me!

The Paleo-way is a method of eating foods that our ancient ancestors would have foraged for, hunted and gathered. Why on earth, with all of the modern advancements and technology available, would we want to regress to eating like a caveperson? Well, with modern advancements have come modern problems.

The average diet today is full of health hazards. Obesity, disease, and digestive issues can all be traced back to the poor diet that is commonly ingested by the masses. These problems became prevalent after the agricultural revolution. So, the idea is that if we go back to a more simplistic, ancient way of eating, we can rid ourselves of the modern problems caused by contemporary developments in agriculture. There is no definite answer as to whether or not this is the reason why we are a fat, disease ridden population. Yet, we can see the benefit in going back to eating the things that we were biologically designed to process.

Grains and legumes (at least most of them), processed foods and oils, sugars and dairy are all foods that we began eating after the agricultural revolution. These are all items that we leave behind, following in our hunter-gatherer relatives' footsteps. Hey, at least you can go to the Farmer's market or grocery store instead of battling a saber toothed tiger on your way to pick up tonight's dinner.

My wife, Elena, drools over a huge bowl of salad. What tickles *my* salivary glands are large pieces of meat. I love meat. If there were better meat desserts I would be in heaven. She and I have never quite seen eye to eye on this issue, as she was always vegan and alkaline drawn, and I was a kid in a candy store at the butcher's counter. I do eat many vegetables as well. When I found the Paleo plan it just made sense to me

Chapter 1: Alkalize with an Ancient Twist

and it was extremely easy to prepare. Chicken salad and tuna salad were always on my menu!

Ela jumped on the prehistoric bandwagon as well. She was very healthy as a vegan, but the lack of animal fats and protein was taking a toll on her. She was having problems with menopause. I had also noticed that she was having to put in long hours at work because she was having issues with thinking and concentration. We finally visited a naturopathic Chinese doctor and he examined Ela's case. He actually told her that her body will benefit from small portions of meat and fish. Since Ela is not big on red meat, we decided to add more fresh fish and seafood as well as organic chicken to her diet.

Elena's health issues (as well as hair loss) began to fix themselves after we decided to try combining our nutritional perspectives. We were so ecstatic!

In our meeting of the minds, we realized that only a few things would need to be changed in order to Paleo-tize her alkaline lifestyle. In order to combine the two and yield the highest results, the 20% non-alkaline foods would now be focused on meat and eggs. We needed to negate all grains and grasses from her alkaline diet. Also tossed out the vegan window were all legumes and beans. Ahhhh no more soy makes me a happy Paleo boy! (of course, I allow her to have her strictly vegan style days, especially now that I know she is healthy). I believe that you can create your own diet and combine different dietary approaches. If soy and legumes work fine with your stomach, there is no need to follow this 100% strict Paleo band wagon. Listen to your body and give it what it needs.

So, in addition to the alkaline list, I am proud to present you with the Paleo list! Hey it may only be twenty percent, but I will take what I can get!!

Chapter 1: Alkalize with an Ancient Twist

- Organic, cage-free, free-range eggs
- Wild caught fish
- Lean cuts of grass-fed meat

**Rule of thumb: THERE SHOULD BE NO INDREDIENTS ON THE LABEL.

As a Paleo fan, I love the fact that you can eat typical lunches or dinners for breakfast. This helps me keep variety in my meals! An added bonus for sure.

It sounds overwhelming at first. When in actuality, it is very simple. If I can do it you can. I am a simple kind of guy. These Alkaline-Paleo guidelines were super easy for me to follow. Ela is a stickler for detail, I like a no-frills approach; once again this nutritional marriage proved itself to be a match made in heaven.

So, now that you know what you CAN eat (you understand the basic outline and allowable ingredients), let us move to the recipes. The recipes we have laid out for you all include meat (small amounts though); allowing us to showcase the Paleo-Alkaline twist.

Like we said in the description and the introduction, this book is about combining two different dietary approaches without becoming 100% alkaline zealot. We want balance, right?

Your everyday meal plan will also include meals without the meat/Paleo. Remember that the twenty percent consists of meat, so, if you have 3-5 meals in a day you only want a small percentage of each to be Paleo-laden. You can also consider having a larger portion meat in one or a couple of your meals and vegan alkaline meals for the rest of the day. Create whatever suits you and your lifestyle. If you are a fitness person, this alkaline paleo lifestyle will keep you energized and toned up.

Chapter 1: Alkalize with an Ancient Twist

Keeping your snacks and drinks strictly high alkaline will help too. Mix and match as you please, just be sure to stick to 80-70/20-30 as closely as you can!

One more thing- water! If you can't stand drinking pure water, we suggest you infuse it with fruits and herbs.

When having meat, make it 20% of your plate. The rest 80% should be alkaline veggies or other alkaline/Paleo friendly ingredients. This is really easy to do when you get used to salads and massive veggie stir fries that you can spice up with a bit of meat and fish.

You will find more tips and recipes in your free bonus eBook that you can claim at:

www.holisticwellnessbooks.com/bonus

Chapter 2 Alkaline Paleo Breakfasts to Start Your Day with a Bang

Breakfast can definitely be the most important meal of the day. The first meal sets the tone for what your body will be craving for the remainder of your waking hours. If you choose a Paleo-infused meal, you will get your proteins and healthy fats in right out of the gate! Begin your morning with one of these tasty Paleo-pumped recipes that are full of alkalinity as well. Aside from the actual recipes, we have also included our nutritional wellness tips so that you can create your own healthy dishes. It's really easy once you understand the rules of Paleo and Alkalinity.

Chapter 2 Alkaline Paleo Breakfasts to Start Your Day with a Bang

Recipe #1 Alkalinity Scramble

This tasty egg dish is quick to put together. Simple to prepare and mouth-watering! Our sons love it too!

Ingredients: serves 2

- 4 organic eggs
- 1-1 ½ cups spinach
- ½ cup sliced or chopped mushrooms
- ½ cup chopped onion
- 1 chopped or minced garlic clove
- 1 TBSP chopped basil
- ½ red bell pepper chopped
- ½ tsp salt
- 1 TBSP coconut oil
- ½ tsp cayenne (optional)

Preparation

1. Whisk the eggs in a bowl.
2. In a frying pan, heat oil to medium (or medium high) and then add pepper and onion. Cook for 2 minutes.
3. Add in the eggs, spinach, mushroom, garlic, and basil.
4. Cook and stir until eggs are done. Sprinkle with salt and cayenne.

Chapter 2 Alkaline Paleo Breakfasts to Start Your Day with a Bang

<u>Our tips:</u>

You can also use olive oil if you wish. We are both great fans of coconut oil. There is no need to use acid-forming margarines and butters. Switch to good oils: coconut oil (also excellent in smoothies), avocado oil, and olive oil are our recommendations.

Craving sugar and sweets? Take 1 tablespoon of coconut oil. It will prevent the cravings. Try it- it really works. Coconut oil offers us good and healthy fats that we need to stimulate our metabolism.

You can also experiment with herb and garlic infused oils. Organic olive oil (cold-pressed) is great for that. You can also use it in veggie smoothies to add to its nutritional value.

Coconut oil on the other hand is great for desserts and you can infuse it with cinnamon or nutmeg. Kids love it!

Chapter 2 Alkaline Paleo Breakfasts to Start Your Day with a Bang

Recipe#2 Belly Breakfast

I, James, adore bacon. If bacon had asked for my hand in marriage, I would have had to seriously think about it (not too sure if Elena would like it though). This recipe will curb a craving for chemical-laden bacon, while providing healthy fats and alkaline veggies. You will not miss a thing! I love this breakfast before hitting the gym. It gives me all I need to successfully complete my workout!

Ingredients: serves 2

- ¼ lb. pork belly sliced thin or pancetta (ask the butcher to do it, tastes like bacon but healthier!)
- ½ onion diced
- ½ bell pepper diced
- 3 asparagus spears diced
- 1 ½ cups spinach
- 1 tablespoon coconut oil (may not be necessary depending
- ½ teaspoon nutmeg
- 1 teaspoon cumin
- 1 tablespoon diced cilantro
- 1 tablespoon diced parsley
- Pinch of salt
- 2 cups favorite salad greens (we use dandelion)
- Big squeeze of lemon juice for the salad greens
- 2 eggs

Chapter 2 Alkaline Paleo Breakfasts to Start Your Day with a Bang

Preparation

1. Put egg and spices in a separate bowl and whisk well, set off to the side

2. Melt the coconut oil in a frying pan over medium. Fry up the pork. When it is cooked fully and browned, remove and allow to drain on paper towels. Leave the rest of the oil in the pan.

3. Add and sauté the asparagus for three minutes, then add the bell pepper and onion cooking for three more minutes.

4. Mix in the spinach, pork, and egg. Cook for 4-5 minutes, until the egg is set, flipping every so often. Divide into two servings and top with cilantro/parsley. Serve with greens and add a squeeze of lemon.

Additional tips- make sure you add all kinds of spices and herbs to your shopping list. These are both alkaline and paleo friendly and will transform every dish you make. They will also provide you with a taste of variety. Our number one recipe for health and dieting success- spice it up as much as possible!

Do you need more Alkalinity? Have a glass of green juice first thing in the morning. It will wake you up- seriously! Green juices are now our "natural green caffeine". They also reduce food cravings and help you stick to your planned serves. They make you feel good and energized first thing in the morning and make the process of breakfast preparation a really nice ritual.

Many people don't like green juices and can't even stand the idea of drinking it on an empty stomach. We were there. It all comes down to getting used to it. Life is all about making choices. Sometimes we must do things that we don't really enjoy only to achieve higher goals. This is the reason many people go to work, right? So no more excuses, make sure you get your greens and do a 30 days "juicing in the morning" challenge. We are not talking about juice cleanse, this is our "healthy maintenance idea". You can have your balanced alkaline-paleo breakfast as always. But first...juice! You can thank us later.

Simple recipe:

Juice 1 cup kale + 1 cup spinach + 1 apple to taste + half inch ginger + 1 lime + 2 carrots + 1 cucumber.

This recipe is great for weight loss and quick energy as you are feeding your body with zillions of nutrients!

Chapter 2 Alkaline Paleo Breakfasts to Start Your Day with a Bang

Recipe#3 Salmon-y Sliders

We serve this breakfast anytime we have company. Everyone loves it. It is interesting and so yummy! It is my (Ela's) favorite as she loves fish of all kind. You can do as I do, and use it for a lunch as well!

Ingredients: serves 2

- 8 Portobello mushrooms (caps only)
- 4 eggs
- 4 ounces smoked salmon
- A few handfuls of spinach
- ½ each onion and cucumber thinly sliced
- Cayenne pepper to taste
- 2-3 Tablespoons coconut oil

Preparation

1. Using a large frying pan or skillet melt 2 tablespoons of coconut oil over medium heat. Add the mushroom caps, face down, and turn to medium low. Cook for 5 min. Remove and set on paper towels to drain.
2. Fry the eggs in the same pan over medium for five minutes or until set.
3. Set up your siders. Put one mushroom cap face up, then add the egg, a little salmon, and sprinkle with cayenne. Then add the spinach, onion and cucumber. Top with another cap face down.

You may find that one is enough, if you have a smaller appetite!

Chapter 2 Alkaline Paleo Breakfasts to Start Your Day with a Bang

If you want to make it more alkaline, serve some tomato, carrot and bell pepper slices on side. Raw veggies are always good and a must for any alkaline-Paleo fan.

Chapter 2 Alkaline Paleo Breakfasts to Start Your Day with a Bang

Recipe #4 Paleo-packed Peppers

This recipe will give you a vegetable kick start, while providing you with some of your Paleo for the day. These peppers are delectable! We had never contemplated using stuffed peppers for breakfast. Such a great way to start the day!

Ingredients: serves 2

- 2 bell peppers any color
- 4 organic free range eggs
- 1 c. mushrooms
- 1 c. broccoli florets
- ½ c. kale
- ½ teaspoon cayenne (omit if you do not like the spice)
- Salt/pepper (to your liking)

Preparation

1. Chop/dice your veggies (not peppers).
2. Set oven to 375 Fahrenheit (190 Celsius) and allow to preheat.
3. Whisk your eggs, seasoning, and vegetables in a bowl.
4. Carefully cut bell peppers in half (top to bottom), and remove stems and ribs/seeds.
5. Lay bell peppers on a cookie sheet, open side up, like a bowl. Use ¼ egg mixture in each. Add more vegetables if the mix does not fill it up all of the way.
6. Bake for 35 min or so, checking to make sure the eggs are cooked.

Chapter 2 Alkaline Paleo Breakfasts to Start Your Day with a Bang

Recipe#5 Apple-Sausage Squash Salad

Nothing beats the smell of home cooked meals (James just said, "Except when you get to eat one!"). The aroma of this meal always has him sitting at the table, fork in hand, before it is even ready.

Ingredients: serves 4

- 1 lb. sliced chicken or pork sausage
- 1 green tart (granny smith) apple (chopped)
- 3 cups butternut squash chopped (if fresh cook it, or use frozen)
- 1 tsp garlic powder
- ½ tsp each cinnamon and nutmeg
- Enough spinach or leafy greens for a small plate of salad x4 (about 1 c. each)

Preparation

1. In a large frying pan brown the sausage and apple over medium. When the sausage is done, drain and set aside.

2. Put your squash in the pan and heat over medium low until warm. Sprinkle with the spices and stir in the sausage/apple mix.

3. Serve over salad. The simple one that we recommend when you are pressed for time, is a cup of spinach leaves with a few cucumber and tomato slices spiced up with a few drizzles of herb infused olive oil, if you can also add avocado slices, you will be hitting Alkalinity first thing in the morning and keep your stomach full and satisfied. There is no reason to be a martyr and live only on greens. Try our breakfast and enjoy the pleasure of balanced eating!

Chapter 2 Alkaline Paleo Breakfasts to Start Your Day with a Bang

Recipe#6Breakfast Bake

This next dish satiates my desire for a baked breakfast casserole. Just like mom used to make! It is full of alkaline vegetables and healthy eggs!

Ingredients: serves 4

- 1 tablespoon coconut oil
- ½ cup bell pepper (chopped)
- 1/2 cup onion (chopped)
- 1 cup spinach
- 2 cups kale (chopped and de-ribbed)
- ½ zucchini chopped
- 8 organic eggs
- 1/2 cup almond milk
- Salt/pepper/crushed red pepper (as much as you like)

    Preparation

1. Set oven to 350 Fahrenheit (175 Celsius). Whisk eggs and milk in a bowl. Season with salt/peppers.
2. Heat a large cast iron skillet over medium with the coconut oil. Cook your onion and peppers for 3 min, the onion will be clear when it is ready.
3. Put in the kale and cook 5 min.
4. Add zucchini, spinach, and eggs, cooking 4 more min.
5. Now put in the oven to bake for 12-15 min. It must be cooked through.
6. Enjoy!

Chapter 2 Alkaline Paleo Breakfasts to Start Your Day with a Bang

Recipe#7 Spicy Sweet Potatoes

I, Elena, make this dish every weekend! I love the spiciness combined with the sweet potatoes. I know you will love it too!

Ingredients: serves 2

- 2 sweet potatoes (cubed)
- 1 chopped onion
- 1 teaspoon cayenne
- 1 chopped, seeded jalapeno
- 1 bell pepper chopped and seeded
- ½ c. grape or cherry tomatoes chopped in half
- 2 TBSP chopped cilantro
- 2 tsp. cumin
- 2 eggs
- 2 TBSP coconut oil

Preparation

1. Heat coconut oil, medium heat, in a frying pan. Add the potatoes, jalapeno onions, and seasonings. Put a lid on it and cook until soft, about 5 min.
2. Take the lid off and allow it to brown for 3 min.
3. Put in all other ingredients, except the eggs. Allow to cook 3 more min, stirring constantly.
4. In the middle of the pan, use a spoon to make a crater in the middle and crack the eggs into it. Put the lid back on and cook three minutes longer (or until eggs look done).

Chapter 2 Alkaline Paleo Breakfasts to Start Your Day with a Bang

Recipe #8 Berry Beefy

Ok, this is James' absolute favorite breakfast. The first time he made it, I had the "you have got to be kidding me" look on my face. He surprised me for sure, and you will be surprised as well. It is so tasty! To be honest, I am not a beef person but for this one, I will make an exception...

Ingredients: serves 4

- 1 lb. super lean ground beef
- 2 tablespoons coconut oil
- 4 cups blueberries
- Cinnamon to taste

    Preparation

1. Heat a frying pan to medium with coconut oil. Add ground beef and brown till almost done. Sprinkle with a few shakes of cinnamon.
2. Turn off heat and mix in the blueberries. Keep in the pan and stir for 2 min.
3. Serve and enjoy!

Chapter 2 Alkaline Paleo Breakfasts to Start Your Day with a Bang

Recipe #8 Yummy Shrimp Veggie Stir-Fry

Here comes another recipe that Elena loves. It's easy to digest and full of nutrients and healthy proteins. (James finds zucchini a bit boring, but thanks to yummy shrimps in this recipe, he got used to it).

Ingredients: serves 2

- 1 cup of shrimps (peeled and ready to eat)
- 1 garlic clove, minced
- 2 big zucchini, cubed into small pieces or sliced
- 1 red bell pepper, diced
- Pinch of Himalaya Salt
- Coconut oil
- 1 teaspoon of rosemary herb
- Pinch of curry and chili powder
- 1 cup of mushrooms

Preparation

1. Heat a frying pan to medium with coconut oil (about 2 tablespoons).
2. Add shrimps and then zucchini, ball pepper and mushrooms.
3. Stir fry adding some garlic, salt and spiced.
4. Make sure zucchini is nicely done-not too raw but also not too soft.
5. Serve and enjoy! We recommend you sprinkle over some lemon juice to make this recipe more alkaline.

Chapter 2 Alkaline Paleo Breakfasts to Start Your Day with a Bang

Recipe#9 Simple Oregano Tuna Stir Fry

We love Italian spices. This recipe will help you love the alkaline-paleo diet first thing in the morning. Just try it yourself!

Ingredients: serves 2

- 2 cans of tuna
- 2 garlic cloves, minced
- 4 tomatoes, sliced and chopped
- 2 tablespoons of almond powder
- 1 tablespoon of fresh oregano
- 1 cup of mushrooms
- A few onion slices
- One small bell pepper, finely chopped
- Olive oil and Himalaya salt

Preparation
1. Heat a frying pan to medium with olive oil.
2. Add garlic and onion. Stir fry for a couple of minutes.
3. Then add mushrooms and bell pepper. Carry on stir frying for a few minutes until soft.
4. Now add tuna and mix well. Add oregano and keep stir frying. You may add a bit more of olive oil.
5. Spice up with some oregano and almond powder. You will feel like eating pizza again!

The key to success is transforming the dishes you love into new, healthy ones. We oftentimes crave pizza and pasta because we want flavors. Simply stir-fry some veggies with oregano and almond powder or other powdered nuts and give yourself this amazing healthy alkaline paleo pleasure.

*****

Chapter 2 Alkaline Paleo Breakfasts to Start Your Day with a Bang

We very often let our bodies rest from animal protein. It's easy for me (Elena) but a bit of a challenge for James, he loves his meat. However, I very often tell him that our Paleolithic ancestors also had no-meat periods. They were not only hunters, but also gatherers, right? I never get it why so many Paleo people stuff themselves with meat. Not long ago, I realized that I want to help Paleo people find healthy, alkaline balance and follow the Paleolithic philosophy at the same time. Don't be afraid to become a gatherer!

To learn how to achieve balance in your diet, don't forget about your free bonus:

http://www.holisticwellnessbooks.com/bonus

Chapter 2 Alkaline Paleo Breakfasts to Start Your Day with a Bang

Recipe#10 Vegan Paleo Breakfast

We love this simple raw breakfast in the summer. We usually spend summers in the South of Spain and it can be really, really hot there.

Ingredients: serves 2

- Half cup of almonds
- One cup of blueberries (these are full of antioxidants)
- One apple, cut into slices
- 1 banana, sliced
- Half cup of dried fruits of your choice (make sure they're sugar free)
- 2 cups of almond milk and a bit of coconut milk or cream for the top
- Cinnamon to spice up
- OPTIONAL: 1 teaspoon of organic spirulina or chlorella powder
    Preparation
    Simply mix all the ingredients in a bowl.

Almond milk and coconut milk are both alkaline and Paleo. This breakfast is moderately alkaline and will keep your stomach full. We also love it when we crave something sweet. Fruit is a natural, healthy treat to fall back on.

Chapter 3: Lasting Lunches: Alkaline with a Splash of Paleo

For some, lunch is a pain; you have to stop your momentum in getting things done to fuel the body and mind. For others, it is a welcomed break in the day. Either way, these Alkaline-Paleo lunches will make your stomach full and your mouth happy!

Chapter 3: Lasting Lunches: Alkaline with a Splash of Paleo

Recipe#11 Salmon Salad Sandwiches with Simple Salad on the Side

We were big fans of tuna salad sandwiches. This recipe allowed us to rid our fridge of mayonnaise and still curb the craving. It replaces bread with sweet potato slices!

Ingredients: serves 2-3

- 1 lb. salmon fillet=1.5 cups salmon for your salad
- salt/pepper to taste
- ½ lemon's juice
- ½ lemon's zest
- 1 stalk of celery, chop well
- 1.5 teaspoons dill, fresh chop well
- 1 tablespoon extra-virgin olive oil
- Small handful of baby spinach for each sandwich

Preparation

1. Season salmon. Bake in a preheated oven, 350 Fahrenheit (157 Celsius) for about 10 min. It will be flaky when done.
2. Put in a mixing bowl.
3. Add in the all other ingredients and mix well with a fork.

Chapter 3: Lasting Lunches: Alkaline with a Splash of Paleo

Recipe#12 Sweet Potato Bread

- 1 large sweet potato (Works better with short wide ones as opposed to long/skinny) sliced ¼ inch thick
- 4 TBSP coconut oil
- ¼ tsp each: paprika and cumin
- 1 tsp garlic powder
- 1 pinch of salt

1. Heat oven (450 Fahrenheit or: 230 Celsius)).
2. Put a wire rack on a baking sheet.
3. In a bowl, mix the spices up with a fork.
4. Using a large bowl or a large zip lock bag, coat the sweet potato in the coconut oil. Add the spices and coat well. Put on the rack.
5. Bake for 35-40 min. Top with more salt if you like.

Now to assemble your sandwiches! Take one piece of "bread" and put a large scoop of salmon salad on it. Top with spinach and another slice of "bread." Serve with salad below!

Chapter 3: Lasting Lunches: Alkaline with a Splash of Paleo

Recipe#13 Simple Salad

Ingredients

- 1 bunch kale, torn
- ¼ cup raw almonds, chopped
- Half of an avocado, chopped
- 3 tbsp. coconut oil, melted
- Pinch of cayenne
- Pinch of sea salt
- Juice of half a lemon
- Fresh pepper

    Preparation

1. Mix salt, cayenne, oil, lemon, and pepper in a small bowl with a fork.
2. Toss the avocado and kale with the dressing and serve with sandwiches.

Recipe#14 Carne Asada with Kale Chips n' Spinach Guacamole

We adore Mexican food! We love nachos and carne asada. This is our go to meal anytime we want some south of the border flavor.

Ingredients: serves 2-4

Crockpot Carne:

- Approx. 2 lb. lean chuck roast
- 1 orange and 2 limes juiced
- ¼ cup evoo
- ½ cup chopped cilantro
- 2 tsp crushed red pepper
- 5 crushed, chopped or minced garlic cloves
- 2 tsp oregano
- ½ tsp cumin
- 4 green onion bulbs chopped or 1 shallot
- 1 teaspoon sea salt

Preparation

1. Rinse your beef and trim all visible fat. Allow to dry ½ hour.
2. Put the other ingredients in food processor. Simply pulse for a min.
3. Put in crockpot. Coat the meat, rubbing it with the marinade.
4. Put about 1/3 cup of water in the bottom of your crockpot.
5. Cook on high for about 5 hours. Slice across grain.

Chapter 3: Lasting Lunches: Alkaline with a Splash of Paleo

Serve slices on 2 stacked kale chips, dolloped with guac.

Chapter 3: Lasting Lunches: Alkaline with a Splash of Paleo

Recipe#15 Guac

- 2 avocados (peeled and pitted)
- 1 large lime (juice)
- 1 cucumber
- 8 c. spinach chopped
- ½ c. cilantro chopped
- ½ cup chopped onion
- 1 tsp. cumin

1. Put all, except cucumber and onion, into blender/processor and mix well. Stir the chopped cucumber and onion into the mix by hand.
2. Put in the fridge.

Chapter 3: Lasting Lunches: Alkaline with a Splash of Paleo

Recipe#16 Kale Chips

- 2 bunches of kale
- 3-4 tablespoons olive oil
- Salt (as much as you like)
- Cayenne (if you want them spicy)

1. Preheat the oven to 300 Fahrenheit (150 Celsius). Remove the rib by slicing top to bottom on each side of it. Then cut each side in half if they are long. If they are short then leave whole (you want to put the carne on top so the leaves will be longer than normal kale chips). 3-4 inches each will work.
2. Wash and dry the leaves, drying is very important: use paper towels or clean towels if needed.
3. I then put the kale, half at a time, in a large bowl or zip lock. Then put in half the oil with each batch, massaging with hands to coat.
4. Lay out on baking sheets and do not overlap. Season.
5. Put sheets in the oven and bake until crispy. Normally I rotate the trays after about 5 min. They usually take 3 min. longer. Do not allow them to brown. They taste nasty! When they are crisp, remove from oven. Transfer onto to paper towels to cool.

Now use two stacked on top of each other, put a thin slice of carne and some guac on top. Do not place the meat on the chip until you are going to put it in your mouth. I usually serve the meat and guac on plates and then give each person a separate serving of chips.

******

Chapter 3: Lasting Lunches: Alkaline with a Splash of Paleo

Recipe #17 Soup n' Souper-Salad

Soup and salad is a classic way to eat lunch. This chicken soup is delicious. It is mild in flavor and will balance the addictive tangy, flavor-packed salad.

Ingredients: serves 2

Prepare salad first (at least a few hours ahead)

Souper-salad:

- 1/2 head cabbage (red) shred
- 1 ½ cups kale (chopped)
- ½ red onion (slice thin)
- ½ cup radishes sliced
- ½ sliced cucumber
- 1 cup raw (not pasteurized) sauerkraut
- 2 sliced green onions
- 3 tbsp chopped mint
- 3 tbsp coconut oil
- 2 tbsp apple cider vinegar
- 1 tbsp maple syrup
- 2 teaspoons Dijon mustard
- ½ tsp cayenne

Preparation

1. Put all of the veggies in a bowl.

Chapter 3: Lasting Lunches: Alkaline with a Splash of Paleo

2. Whisk together the ingredients for the dressing in another bowl.

3. Add the dressing and stir to combine. Allow to set a few hours. Serve with soup!

Chapter 3: Lasting Lunches: Alkaline with a Splash of Paleo

Recipe#18 Soup

- 1 quart chicken broth
- ½ lb. shredded cooked chicken (leftovers work well)
- 1 large rib celery, dice or chop
- 1 large carrot, dice or chop
- 1 zucchini, use a grater, peeler or slicer to make noodles
- Salt/pepper to taste (if you like crushed red pepper or cayenne please add)

1. Boil the broth and add the cooked chicken. Turn to low and simmer
2. Put in the carrots and celery for 20 min.
3. Now, add noodles and cook 3-4 min longer.

Chapter 3: Lasting Lunches: Alkaline with a Splash of Paleo

Recipe#19 Chicken-Strip Salad

James misses breaded chicken sometimes. Breading in almond meal is a Paleo-acceptable way to prepare chicken. He loves these strips a-top my favorite salad!

Ingredients: serves 2-3

- 1 pound chicken breast (boneless and skinless)
- 1 cup almond meal
- 1 heaping tablespoon paprika
- 1 teaspoon garlic powder
- 1 teaspoon cayenne pepper
- 1 teaspoon coarse ground pepper
- 1 teaspoon salt
- 2 eggs (beat)
- A few tablespoons oil to grease baking sheets

  Preparation

1. Heat your oven (375 Fahrenheit or 190 Celsius)).
2. Cut your chicken into one or two inch wide strips.
3. Mix the meal and spices.
4. Grease baking sheets.
5. Dunk each piece of chicken in the egg and then roll in the meal.
6. Put the chicken on baking sheets in the oven for 25 min or so until crispy and brown.

Make salad and then serve chicken on the salad.

Chapter 3: Lasting Lunches: Alkaline with a Splash of Paleo

Recipe#20 Salad

- 1 lb. baby spinach
- ½ of a lemon (to squeeze)
- ¼ cup coconut oil
- A few splashes of coconut aminos (your preference)
- 1 large avocado, dice
- ¼ cup chopped almonds

1. Wash and dry spinach.
2. Mix all dressing ingredients in bowl and stir in the avocado.
3. Now combine all of the ingredients toss well.

Chapter 3: Lasting Lunches: Alkaline with a Splash of Paleo

Recipe#21 Asian Meatballs with Noodles

This meatball recipe will fill your kitchen with delicious Far East aromas! The noodles are made of zucchini; bring on the alkalinity!

Ingredients: serves 4

Noodle Salad

- 1 large extra-large zucchini
- 2 tablespoons rice vinegar
- 1 teaspoon sesame oil
- ¼ teaspoon red pepper flakes
- ½ teaspoon coconut aminos
- ½ teaspoon ginger powder
- Salt/pepper

1. Take a carrot peeler, peel up your entire zucchini up into noodles. Stir in all of your other ingredients as well. Allow flavors to combine for at least twenty minutes while you prepare the meatball.

Paleo Meatballs

- 2 lbs pork (ground)
- 2 teaspoons salt
- 1 teaspoon coriander
- ½ teaspoon white pepper (use black if you want)
- ½ teaspoon cayenne
- 2 tsp crushed red pepper
- 2 teaspoons fish sauce

Chapter 3: Lasting Lunches: Alkaline with a Splash of Paleo

- 1 tablespoon sesame oil
- 2 Tablespoons coconut aminos
- 1 ½ piece of ginger, grated
- 1/3 cup cilantro (chop)
- 4 scallion bulbs (chop)

1. Mix the pork, salt, coriander, peppers, fish sauce, oil, aminos, ginger, cilantro and scallion in a bowl. Sprinkle spices all around, do not dump them in.
2. Squish up with your hands to combine all well. Do not squish meat too much or it may toughen when cooked.
3. Cover two cookie sheets with parchment paper: one for cooking and one for cooling. Roll the meatballs (they should be about a tablespoon).
4. Use a large skillet and heat to medium high. Add your meatballs. You will have to make a few batches because they need room in order to brown.
5. They will cook for a total of about twenty minutes. Turn them three times during the cooking process. Transfer to the other baking sheets. Until they are all done.

Chapter 3: Lasting Lunches: Alkaline with a Splash of Paleo

Recipe#22 Simple Vegan Paleo Salad

We love seaweed like kombu or wakame. These are both alkaline and Paleo friendly and we recommend you start using them in your salads. Like we have already mentioned before, it's good to do a few days without meat every now and then. This recipe should give you some ideas as for vegan Paleo options. It's all about healthy variety, right?

Ingredients (serves 2)

- A few square inches of wakame
- A few square inches of kombu
- One cup of radish
- 2 avocados, sliced and pitted
- Half cup of almonds
- 2 tablespoons of chia seeds
- ¼ cup raisins (raisins and onion are an excellent taste combination!)
- Half onion, minced
- 2 big tomatoes
- Olive oil
- Juice of 1 lemon
- Himalaya salt

OPTIONAL: if you really need some animal protein, add tuna or raw shrimps /salmon

Preparation

1. Soak wakame and kombu in water (you may want to slice it first) for about 10m mins.
2. In the meantime, mix other ingredients in a big bowl.
3. Add olive oil and lemon juice.
4. Finally, mixed in wakame and kombu.
5. Enjoy, we do!

Chapter 4 Delectable Alkaline Dinners

Ending the day on a good note is important in our home, as I am sure it is in yours. Choosing to eat your meaty meal at the end of the day can be a welcomed treat, especially if you are like James and need motivation in the form of meat to push you through.

This dinner recipe sounds funny but tastes delicious. Bison adds a great flavor to these balls. The alkaline roasted vegetables compliment the flavor well!

Chapter 4 Delectable Alkaline Dinners

Recipe#23 Bison Balls and Roast Veggies

Ingredients: serves 4-6

- 2 pounds ground bison (you can use whatever lean ground meat you like)
- 1/2 an onion, chop
- 1 ½ teaspoons sea salt
- 1 teaspoon cumin
- ½ teaspoon cayenne
- ½ teaspoon black pepper
- 2 cups spinach, chop and pack tightly
- ½ cup cilantro
- 2 beaten eggs

Preparation

1. Set oven to 400 Fahrenheit (200 Celsius). Cover baking sheets with parchment paper.
2. Mix everything in a bowl with hands.
3. Roll into balls, about 1 heaping tablespoon of mix per ball.
4. Bake 25 min. They need to be browning and cooked through.

Recipe#24 Roast Veggies

- 1 head cauliflower, chop
- 1 squash (which ever you like), peel and cube
- 2 chopped beets
- 1 large zucchini
- 2 large carrots
- 2 tablespoons coconut oil
- 2 tablespoons fresh parsley, chop
- 1 teaspoon cayenne
- 1 tablespoon black pepper
- 1 tablespoon rosemary

Preparation

1. Set oven to 400 Fahrenheit (200 Celsius).
2. Mix all veggies in a bowl, but keep zucchini separate. Toss the mixed veggies with most of the oil save a little bit.
3. Spread the vegetables out on a cookie sheet and sprinkle with salt and pepper.
4. Roast for 20 min.
5. Coat zucchini and season with salt/pepper.
6. Add zucchini to the other vegetables and stir, roasting ten more min.
7. Sprinkle with rosemary and parsley.

Chapter 4 Delectable Alkaline Dinners

Recipe#25 Barbeque Chicken and Coleslaw

This dinner is great for summer! Even in the dead of winter it is delicious and will help you to have a taste of July in January! We love this coleslaw and receive nothing but compliments on it.

Ingredients: serves 2-4

- 1 chicken (whole, guts removed)
- 1 onion, slice
- 3 teaspoons paprika
- 1 teaspoon sea salt
- 1 teaspoon onion powder
- 1 teaspoon thyme
- 1 teaspoon white pepper
- 1 teaspoon cayenne
- 5 minced garlic cloves
- 1 teaspoon black pepper

Preparation

1. Dry chicken thoroughly.
2. Put onions in the bottom of the crockpot.
3. Put the chicken on the onions.
4. Mix all of the ingredients in another bowl. This will be your rub, using your hands massage the chicken with the seasonings (outside and inside).
5. Cook set to low setting for at least six hours or until done.

Chapter 4 Delectable Alkaline Dinners

Recipe#26 Coleslaw

- 2 cups green cabbage, shred
- 2 cups red cabbage, shred
- 2 bell peppers sliced thin
- 4 carrots, julienned
- 2 cups bok choy
- 3 tablespoons chives chopped
- 2 tablespoons coconut aminos
- 2 tablespoons coconut oil
- ½ lemon to squeeze for juice
- 1 tablespoon sesame oil
- 3 teaspoons freshly grated ginger root
- 2 teaspoons tahini
- Pinch of sea salt

Preparation

1. Mix all of the veggies in a bowl. In another bowl whisk your dressing ingredients. Pour over vegetables and coat well. Serve it as soon as you toss it!

Chapter 4 Delectable Alkaline Dinners

Recipe #27 Italian Beef

I, Ela, had an Italian grandmother and I miss her cooking oh so much. When I make this recipe, my kitchen smells like grandma's did, so many years ago. I have taken out the pasta and replaced it with my favorite: zucchini noodles (I cannot get enough of these).

Ingredients: serves 2-4

- 4 lb. round roast
- Few tablespoons of oil (olive or coconut)
- 2 onions, slice
- 5 cloves garlic, minced
- 2 teaspoons garlic powder
- 2 tablespoons oregano divided in half
- 3 c. raw baby carrots

Preparation

1. Sear the roast on both sides in a dutch-oven, using high heat. Make sure that it browns well on both sides before flipping. Add some oil, turn down to medium high, and brown on all sides for a few minutes. Take out the roast and set aside.

2. Turn the heat even lower, to medium. Put in both garlic and onion. Cook for three or four minutes.

3. Sprinkle the meat with oregano and garlic powder, then put back in the pan.

4. Pour in a cup of cold water, put the lid on and simmer over medium low for three and a half hours or so. If you need, add a bit more water. I might check every hour. After two hours, put in

Chapter 4 Delectable Alkaline Dinners

the baby carrots, sprinkle with the rest of the garlic powder and oregano.

5. When done, take out the meat and slice. Serve over noodles below with carrots on the side.

Recipe#28 Zucchini Noodles

- 2 medium zucchinis
- 1 cup baby spinach per serving
- 1 tablespoon olive oil
- 1 garlic clove, minced
- Salt/pepper

1. Use a box style grater using the big holes. Chop off the tips of the zucchini.
2. Push along the grater with pushing the length of the zucchini, making long noodles.
3. Use a pan and heat the oil to medium. Fry the noodles for a few minutes until tender.

Place spinach on the plate, then a serving of noodles, and finally the beef and carrots.

Chapter 4 Delectable Alkaline Dinners

Recipe#29 Topped Tilapia with Kale Salad

We adore tilapia. It is replaceable with other white fish in this recipe. I sometimes make a double recipe of the pesto, as it is a favorite in our home and very versatile!

Ingredients (serves 2)

- 4 tilapia filets
- 1 tablespoon olive oil
- 2 cloves garlic
- 2 tablespoons water
- 30 basil leaves
- 1 inch chunk of zucchini (peel)

    Preparation

1. Blend in food processor or blender all but tilapia in blender, taa daah pesto sauce.
2. Spread over tilapia.
3. Allow oven to preheat to 400 Fahrenheit (200 Celsius)
4. Bake for 20 minutes.

Chapter 4 Delectable Alkaline Dinners

Recipe#30 Krispy Kale Salad

- 2 bunches kale, stems removed and torn
- 1 c. fennel, chop
- 10 baby radishes, shred
- 2 tablespoons olive oil
- Pinch of sea salt
- Big squeeze of lemon

Mix well in a bowl, serve alongside tilapia.

When you want some comfort food and do not want to fall off the wagon, prepare this recipe. The fried chicken and mashed potatoes included are Alkaline-Paleo, but will kill the urge to cheat!

Recipe#31 Chicken, Sprouts, n Spuds

Ingredients: serves 2

Chicken and Sprouts
- 2 chicken leg quarters
- ¼ c. veggie broth
- 1 stalk of Brussels Sprouts (remove stem)
- 1 ½ tablespoon coconut oil
- Salt, black and crushed red pepper to taste
- 3 crushed garlic cloves
- 1 tablespoon olive oil
- 1 lemon to squeeze

Preparation
1. Allow oven to heat to 425 Fahrenheit (220 Celsius)
2. Prepare your sprouts, and then half them.
3. Coat the sprouts in olive oil. Sprinkle with salt/peppers.
4. Season rinsed and dried chicken as well.
5. Put coconut oil in a cast iron skillet and heat over medium to medium-high.
6. When heated, put in the chicken, skin side down. Allow to cook until nice and crunchy. 5-8 min. Do not move them around in the pan.
7. When this is done, flip and do the same for the underside.
8. Add sprouts, ¼ c. broth, and squeeze the lemon in. Mix well.
9. Bake in oven for half of an hour, or until chicken is done.

Recipe#32 Spuds

- 6 sweet potatoes
- 1 ½ cups coconut milk
- 1 tablespoon coconut oil
- 1 tablespoon salt
- 1 teaspoon pepper
- 1 tsp cayenne
- 1 ½ teaspoons curry

1. Chop the potatoes and boil for 18-22 minutes.
2. When soft, drain then mash them, mixing in the other ingredients.

Serve alongside chicken and Brussels.

BONUS CHAPTER: Alkaline Paleo Salads

BONUS CHAPTER: Alkaline Paleo Salads

Recipe#32 Apple and Celery Root Salad

Servings: 2-3

Ingredients

- 1 medium red apple, skin-on and diced
- 2 tablespoons of crashed cashew nuts mixed with 2 tablespoons of coconut oil (our vegan mayo!)
- 1 tablespoon of Dijon Mustard (to our knowledge- this is Paleo acceptable)
- 1 medium sized celery root, peeled and grated
- 4 tablespoons of chopped walnuts
- Paleo Gremolade(1 tablespoon)
- Juice of 1 lemon
- 2 scallions (sliced)
- Half cup of thick coconut yogurt
- Half cup of minced fresh parsley leaves

Method of preparation

1. Toss celery root with diced apples and lemon juice. Then add-in the scallions, walnuts and parsley. Toss again to combine.
2. Mix the gremolade and mayonnaise with coconut yoghurt in another bowl.
3. Add the mayonnaise salad dressing to the apples mixture and then toss to combine.
4. Cover the salad bowl with saran wrap and refrigerate for at least 2-3 hours before serving.

BONUS CHAPTER: Alkaline Paleo Salads

Recipe#33 Samphire Roast Lemon and Hazelnut Salad

Servings: 2-3

Ingredients:
- oz. (180 grams) of Samphire
- Organic maple syrup(1-2 tablespoons)
- 0.881 oz. (25 grams) of hazelnuts
- 1 whole lemon, sliced
- 3 whole radishes
- Olive oil (about 2 tablespoons)

Ingredients for the dressing:
- Paleo maple syrup (1 tablespoon)
- Olive Oil (2 tablespoons)
- Fresh juice of half a lemon
- 2 tablespoons of finely chopped fresh mint leaves

Method of preparation:

1. Preheat an oven to 446 degrees Fahrenheit (230 Celsius). Slice lemon into thin slices.
2. Combine the olive oil and maple syrup in a bowl. Dip the lemon slices in the maple syrup mixture and transfer to a parchment paper lined baking tray.
3. Insert the tray in the oven and roast for 15-20 mins until the lemon slices start to brown.
4. Mix olive oil with maple syrup and lemon juice in a bowl. Whisk well to combine and then add-in the mint leaves to prepare the dressing.
5. Lay the hazelnuts in a baking tray and roast in the oven for 5 minutes.
6. Steam the samphire for 1 minute over a steamer in the meantime and then rinse the leaves under cold water. Drain properly and set aside.

BONUS CHAPTER: Alkaline Paleo Salads

7. Finally, toss the steamed samphire leaves with the roasted lemon slices and hazelnuts. Drizzle the seasoning on top and toss again to serve.

BONUS CHAPTER: Alkaline Paleo Salads

Recipe#34 Green Papaya Salad

Servings: 2

Ingredients

- oz. (50g) of mixed fresh lettuce leaves
- ½ of a green papaya, julienned
- 1 whole radish, sliced
- ½ of a small carrot, julienned
- 2 tablespoons of raw cashew nuts
- 2-3 whole cherry tomatoes, quartered

For the Chilli Dressing

- Coconut vinegar (1 tablespoon)
- Raw honey (1 tablespoon)
- 2 tablespoons of water
- 1 red long chili,(remove the seeds and chop)
- A bit of of fresh lime juice
- 1 tablespoon of Paleo fish sauce
- 1 small clove of garlic, peeled and minced

Method of preparation

1. Toss the julienned carrots and papaya with radish and lettuce leaves. Place in a bowl. Top with the quartered cherry tomatoes and cashews. Set aside.
2. In a separate bowl take the chili slices and add the other ingredients required for the dressing. Whisk to combine.
3. Drizzle the dressing over the salad and serve with lemon wedges.

Recipe#35 Summer Slaw with Tahini Coconut Dressing

Servings: 4

Ingredients for slaw
- 1 head of fennel, cored and sliced
- 1/4th cup of raisins
- 1/4th of a head of purple cabbage, cored and sliced
- Half cup of Thai basil
- 1 bell pepper /remove seeds and slice/

Ingredients for the dressing
- 1 tablespoon of coconut milk
- 2 tablespoons of paleo tahini
- 1-inch of fresh ginger, grated
- 1 teaspoon of paleo raw honey
- Lime juice (use 1 lime)
- 1 teaspoon of sea salt
- Black pepper, to taste

Ingredients for curried cashews
- 1 cup of raw cashew nuts
- 1/4th teaspoon of paprika
- 1 tablespoon of raw coconut oil
- 1 tablespoon of lime juice
- 1 ½ teaspoons of paleo curry powder
- 1/4th teaspoon of chili powder
- 1/4th teaspoon of turmeric powder

Method of preparation

1. To prepare the cashews, heat up 1-2 tablespoons of organic coconut oil in a pan and add the lemon juice and herbs to the oil. Stir for a minute and then drop the cashews in the oil.
2. Stir the nuts in the oil for a minute and transfer to a

BONUS CHAPTER: Alkaline Paleo Salads

parchment paper lined cookie sheet.

3. Bake the nuts in a 350 degrees Fahrenheit (or 175 Celsius) preheated oven for 10-15 minutes. Remove once done and let cool.

4. To prepare the slaw, toss the chopped fennel with cabbage, basil leaves and yellow pepper slices.

5. Whisk all the dressing ingredients until a smooth dressing is formed.

6. Drizzle the dressing over the slaw and drop the raisins and cashew nuts on top to serve.

BONUS CHAPTER: Alkaline Paleo Salads

Recipe#36 Raw Broccoli Slaw

Servings: 4

Ingredients

- 1 cup of carrots(shredded)
- ½ cup of fresh red cherries
- 1½ cups of broccoli florets, shredded
- 3/4th cup of red cabbage, shredded
- ½ cup of thinly sliced red onion
- 1 cup of baby kale leaves

Dressing

- 3 teaspoons of chia seeds
- 4 teaspoon of paleo Dijon mustard
- 6 tablespoon of coconut vinegar
- 6 tablespoons of extra virgin olive oil
- 1/4th cup of raw honey
- 1/4th teaspoon of black pepper
- ½ teaspoon of kosher salt

Method of preparation

1. Process the carrots and broccoli florets in a food processor to shred those. Place in a large bowl. Add the onion slices, cherries, kale leaves and shredded red cabbage.
2. Prepare the dressing by mixing everything in a separate bowl.
3. Drizzle the dressing over the slaw and toss before serving.

BONUS CHAPTER: Alkaline Paleo Salads

Don't forget to pick up your FREE GIFT...

BONUS CHAPTER: Alkaline Paleo Salads

Free Complimentary eBook

Download link:

http://www.holisticwellnessbooks.com/bonus

Problems with your download?

Contact us: elenajamesbooks@gmail.com

Conclusion: Take Positive Action Today!

We provided a basic rundown of the Alkaline and Paleolithic lifestyles. You now have food lists and recipes. The only thing left to do is to start preparing these meals and change your life for the better!

You will notice improvements in all areas. Your brain will flourish! You will have tons of energy, lose weight, and health issues will improve quickly. No longer will you need to implement and search for cures and quick fixes. The answer is in changing your dietary habits!

Vegetable lovers can have their "cake" and eat it too! Meat fanatics will be allowed a nice portion of mouthwatering animal goodness while still alkalizing their bodies! You will love the balance incorporated in this nutritional lifestyle. You will LOVE the results that you will indefinitely see and experience.

By living according to an Alkaline-Paleo blueprint, you are essentially giving your body the fuel it was designed to run on. You will be feeding yourself and your family the foods that your body needs in order to function optimally! Do not waste another day! Get started now, feel the health benefits immediately! Life is short; enjoy it to the fullest by eating Alkaline-Paleo based foods.

To your success,

Elena and James

Follow us at:

www.facebook.com/HolisticWellnessBooks
www.twitter.com/WellnessBooks

Book 2
Paleo Diet for Weight Loss and Health

Get Back to your Paleolithic Roots, Lose Massive Weight and Become a Sexy Paleo Caveman/ Cavewoman!!!

+40 HOT PALEO RECIPES + TIPS INCLUDED!

www.holisticwellnessbooks.com/bonus

By James Adler

Copyright © 2013, 2016

All rights reserved. No part of this publication may be reproduced, stored in a retrieval system, or transmitted, in any form or by any means, electronic, mechanical, photocopying, recording or otherwise without the prior written permission of the author and the publishers.

Introduction

My Paleo Experience

Are you tired of fad diets? Are you looking for a lifestyle transformation? Do you believe that **weight loss** is something more than getting slimmer? How about feeling **amazing** all the time, **radiating energy** and being a **health role model** to other people? If you are not a fan of extremely difficult and restrictive cleansings and fasts but would still like to **holistically detoxify your system**, you **have picked the right book**. It's not about some scientific mumbo jumbo- it's about **a practical approach** with **plenty of recipes to choose** from and fall in love with…it's not about torturing yourself for a few days and then giving up again and again (I have been there myself) but about shifting your focus and making a conscious decision **of body and mind transformation**.

Do you want to join me?

Ten years ago I was feeling ashamed when looking in the mirror. Now I feel proud. I know that it was hard work and dedication but it has totally paid off. I feel **energetic** and **literally bouncing off the walls**. I am 46 years old now and feel much fitter than when I was 20. Many people think that I am a professional athlete. I just tell them my story- **I transformed my body.** You can do it too. I really want to share my passion for **Paleo Diet** with other people and make it easy and doable for them.

My book explains the Paleo-perspective and ancient history behind the newest-oldest diet and how it is a multi-beneficial lifestyle change. The reason why this diet works is because it consists of **what we are biologically designed to eat**; what fuels our bodies to function properly for optimum health. It will show you not only how you can lose weight, gain energy you never thought you could have, and **cure/prevent a plethora of illnesses**.

Included are tips on how to start living Paleo, food lists, recipes, guidelines, and tools that will help you continue to live this way for the rest of your life.

I have always battled with my body in order to maintain a healthy weight. Some diets worked for a time, while others just failed from the beginning. I could lose 30 pounds but would gain it all back, if not more. In this book I am going to share my personal experience with you.

I was plagued with **allergies and asthma** from adolescence. The doctors always blamed my environment. During my late teens, I began experiencing **migraines**, depression, and anxiety. People told me that it was circumstantial, stress related, or just hormones.

About ten years ago, I noticed that an old friend of mine looked amazing. She was fit, looked bright and full of life, vibrant and healthy. She had suffered from many ailments all her life. I had to know, what was her secret? That is when I learned about Paleo diet. I dove right in and never looked back. It all coincided with other things that I attracted into my life: sport, yoga, meditation. I also started to study and investigated the field of nutrition and realized how brainwashed I became. We are constantly being sold an unhealthy lifestyle. Just analyze all the commercials, all over the world it is pretty much the same. Trust me I have lived in different countries and over 4 continents...(Asia is different though). We are all victims of the system where marketers very often try to sell what sells, not what is healthy and sustainable long-term. I felt amazed by my discovery.

Introduction

Thanks to Paleo, I have maintained a weight loss of 40 pounds for nine years, have no allergy/asthma/migraine attacks, and my depression and anxiety are a thing of the past. It will work for you to... all you have to do is eat what we were biologically designed to consume.

DISCLAIMER:

A physician has not written the information in this book. Although Paleo Diet is generally safe to use, you should consult your physician first to check if you can apply it. This book offers a general overview of the Paleo Diet to help you get started on it. For better results, I suggest you consult a dietician specialized in Paleo Diet. If you are suffering from severe obesity, I also suggest you consult with your physician.

Chapter 1 Paleo Lifestyle Made Easy

Welcome Gift
Free Complimentary eBook

Download link:

www.holisticwellnessbooks.com/bonus

Problems with your download?

Contact us: elenajamesbooks@gmail.com

Chapter 1 Paleo Lifestyle Made Easy

Are you looking for the newest, trendiest diet that uses fresh, new ideas and guiding principles to help you lose weight? Do you want to read up on the most contemporary, state of the art program to get lean and energized? If you answered "yes," then the Paleo diet is NOT for you.

Paleo diet is an approach to eating that originated a long time ago, during the Paleolithic era. This time frame started about 2.5 million years ago and ended around 10,000 years before our time. It avoids eating foods that only became part of the human diet after the agricultural revolution. The idea is that diseases like cancer and diabetes started around the same time that we began growing our own foods. The underlying principle is that the hunter-gatherers' diet is the reason why they did not develop such diseases.

While we cannot be sure that diet is what kept them healthy, there is enough research that concludes foods banned from Paleo diets have little or no beneficial nutritional value. They have also been proven to mess up normal hormonal balances, cause inflammation and damage the lining of the gut. Eating Paleo will help to balance our bodies internally, protect the kidneys, protect the digestive tract from destructive proteins like gluten, and keep the liver and pancreas from having to work too hard.

Many names and titles have been given to this age-old eating program: Paleolithic diet, Paleolithic nutrition, Paleo diet, Stone Age diet, caveman diet, and hunter-gatherer diet. Paleo Diet is an effort to go back to eating how we were biologically intended to eat. This method enables us to fuel our bodies properly so that they may function genetic potential and start living healthier immediately. Foods that could be collected and consumed by hunting and gathering are what need to focus on; primal eating at its best.

For me, I like to think of it as a Paleo perspective. It is not an actual diet. It could also be called a template. However you look at it, it is a lifestyle change. The goal is to eat like our ancestors did millions of years ago before the Agricultural Revolution.

Here are seven guidelines in Paleo nutrition that helped me to get a better idea of the principles involved in this primal nutritional practice.

1. **Increase protein intake.**

    15 % of the calories in most diets are from protein. When adhering to Paleo that percentage must be much higher. It should be between 19-35 percent. A large amount of animal protein is required.

2. **Decrease carbohydrate intake and eat foods lower on the glycemic index.**

    Most of the carbs will come from vegetables (and a few fruits). They should take up between 35-45 percent of your daily caloric intake. Most of the foods you will eat will be low on the glycemic index. They will not make your blood sugar spike because they are assimilated slowly.

3. **Increase fiber consumption.**

    Paleos get their fiber from non-starchy vegetables. Vegetables such as these usually contain a fiber content that is around 30 percent higher than processed grain and about eight times higher than even whole grain. Even fruits have more fiber than whole and refined grains.

4. Increase fat intake by eating more monounsaturated and polyunsaturated fats.

You need to do is in combination with a good balance of Omega-3 and Omega-6 fats. It is a common misconception that health is related to how *much* fat you eat, when actually the *type* of fat you eat affects your health. Increase monounsaturated and Omega-3 fats and remove Trans and Omega-6 polyunsaturated fats.

5. Raise potassium, while lowering sodium.

Paleolithic humans consumed foods that were unrefined and fresh. Potassium levels in fresh foods are between 5-10 percent higher than sodium levels. Potassium helps the heart, kidneys, and additional organs function correctly. People who have low potassium levels are susceptible to elevated blood pressure, stroke, and cardiovascular disease. Excessive sodium levels can also cause the same problems. Many modern diets contain two times as much sodium as potassium.

6. Eat more alkaline than acid foods.

When we consume foods, each has either n acid or alkaline effect on your body. Even on a Paleo diet it is necessary to keep this in mind as meat and fish are both acid forming foods. Alkaline-producing foods include most vegetables and fruits. Having an acidic system for a long time can lead to atrophy of the muscle and bone, elevated blood pressure, kidney stones, and trigger things like asthma and allergies.

Please check out the recommended reading at the end of this chapter. You will get the tools to successfully combine the best of paleo diet and the alkaline diet for optimal results.

7. **Increase the intake of vitamins, phytochemicals, minerals, and antioxidants.**

   Whole grains are a poor source of these things. The few minerals and vitamins that are actually in whole grains are not usually processed and absorbed properly by the body. They do not contain vitamin C, vitamin A, or vitamin B12. There truly is no substitute for grass produced and free-range meat, or organic vegetables and fruits.

What foods did the cave men eat? What foods did they hunt and what did they go out and gather? These are two key questions to keep in mind when deciding what TO eat on the Paleo diet.

Basic categories of foods TO consume when eating Paleo:

- Grass-produced meats
- Fish/seafood
- Eggs
- Fresh fruits and vegetables
- Seeds
- Healthful oils (Olive, walnut, flaxseed, macadamia, avocado, coconut)

The foods included on the Paleo diet are foods that our cave-dwelling ancestors would have access to on a regular basis.

Basic categories of what NOT to eat when eating Paleo:

Chapter 1 Paleo Lifestyle Made Easy

- Cereals and grains
- Potatoes
- Legumes
- Sugars
- Processed foods
- Salt
- Dairy
- Refined vegetable oil

Some people do not understand exactly what a legume is. A legume is the seed pod of a plant that is edible. Examples of legumes are:

- beans
- peas
- lentils
- peanuts
- alfalfa
- clover
- carob
- soy
- lupini

Essentially, if a caveman could not have eaten it 10,000 years ago, you cannot eat it now. No consuming packaged foods at all. If it contains chemicals and ingredients that you cannot pronounce, then it is probably not Paleo.

Chapter 2 Losing Weight With Paleo

Eating a Paleo diet takes us back to basics, way back. You may be wondering, "Why if this 'diet' is so old, am I just hearing about it?" All the buzz is being generated because people are stepping away from modern eating habits and feeling better. Paleo nutritional practices are helping people lose weight, have tons of energy, lessen inflammation, clear up skin problems, gain muscle, cure allergies, stop asthma symptoms, get rid of digestive issues, get people off of their diabetes medicines and much more.

As I stated previously, I did not just want to lose weight by eating Paleo. I had a variety of other health problems: headaches, asthma, allergies, anxiety, depression, and acne. Paleolithic nutrition can aid you in ridding yourself of these illnesses along with countless others. Eating Paleo is also a means to prevent Alzheimer's, diabetes, cardiovascular disease, and cancer. All of these problems have a common contributing factor: inflammation.

LOSING WEIGHT- MY PERSONAL EXPERIENCE

How did Paleo help me to lose weight? The easy answer: carbs, calories, caffeine, and my immune system. In order to see how it worked, I needed to know why I ended up getting/being fat in the first place.

<u>1) Eating too many calories causes weight gain.</u>

When eating refined, processed carbs (bread, crackers, chips, rice, cookies, etc.) it is very easy to eat too many calories which leads to weight gain. These foods are full of calories but will not fill you up. That is how we sometimes end up eating too much. These refined carb, calorie dense foods will spike blood sugar. But what goes up will come down, and we are left with a crash in blood sugar. Most of the time it makes you think that you want to eat sweets minutes later (the brain wants the blood sugar to spike again). I know all too often, I have eaten a bowl of spaghetti and garlic bread only to be starving in a half hour!

Protein and fat have been proven to be more filling foods than refined carbohydrates. Meats and fats help to ensure that I do not over eat. They keep me full for a longer period of time than rice or bread. If you eat 300 calories worth of chicken, you will feel fuller longer than if you ate 300 calories worth of chips.

I no longer snacked on calorie rich foods that would leave me hungry for more. I ate three or four meals full of protein and fats in combination with fibrous, nutrient rich vegetables and fruit. I feel for full for hours and consume significantly fewer calories. I no longer have to drink coffee all day long because my blood sugar levels are a lot more stable and my foods are nutrient rich. I get enough energy from my diet alone!

2) Drinking caffeine can make you fat.

Caffeine is a stimulant that creates a highly stressful state in your body. This stress from caffeine encourages your body to create cortisol. Cortisol can mess up digestive processes and causes fat to accumulate around the middle.

Although I did not notice at the time, I was drinking caffeine because processed grains were making me lethargic. They can have an effect on the body that is the equivalent of taking an opiate. Blood sugar crashes are also to blame. Sure there was the occasional late night when I needed a pick-me-up the next morning, but the major cause of my caffeine consumption was due to the grains in my diet.

After removing foods that sent my blood sugar on a roller-coaster ride every day, I stopped needing caffeine. Those grain-induced comatose moments were also gone, so the need to counter-act them with copious amounts of caffeine was no longer there either.

3) My immune system was making me fat.

Wheat, soy, grains and beans contain anti-nutrients that are impossible for our bodies to digest. They contain these elements to deter plants' natural predators from eating them. The result of eating and trying to digest them anyway is digestive distress in the form of: gas, bloating, diarrhea, and worse. All of these results are things people have come to accept as part of eating. Yet, these symptoms are indications that what we are eating is unnatural in relation to digestion.

What could be worse you might ask? Well, those anti-nutrients can stick to the lining of the intestine and cause it to break down. Now food particles escape the intestine and get into the blood stream. It is called, "leaky gut." This causes your immune system to respond to the invader and try to fight it. This can cause eczema, headaches, water-retention, inflammation, and other nasty things.

I cannot stand water retention. It adds to the feeling of being fat. It adds pounds, makes you appear larger in general, and feel bloated in the stomach.

After I removed the grains and legumes that contain anti-nutrients from my diet, my intestines were able to slowly heal. My immune system calmed down. My water retention went away. Eating Paleo was the key.

Taking on a Paleo nutritional perspective allowed me to lose weight, and better yet, keep it off. I no longer ate calorie rich foods that left me wanting more. I no longer needed to drink caffeine to get through my day. My immune system stopped going crazy because my intestines had time to heal. Sure I lost a lot of variety in convenience foods, but I gained a more energetic, healthy, slim self.

CURING MY OTHER AILMENTS

Inflammation is the body's natural response to invaders. I already discussed this problem and how "leaky gut" will lead to weight gain. It may be more important to note that "leaky gut" will lead to major health issues because it causes chronic inflammation. Cancer, asthma, headaches, allergies, arthritis, auto-immune disorders, heart disease, diabetes, depression, Alzheimer's, and osteoporosis are all caused by chronic inflammation. The list literally goes on and on.

Why does inflammation cause so many problems? Inflammation is an immune system response. It is used by the body to battle intruders that are unidentified or already deemed harmful. Well, how could something good cause such a problem? Let me explain it this way, it is like leaving the heater turned up and the thermostat not working. It never turns off when the environment gets to a certain temperature. Yes, you wanted to warm up, but if it never turns off it will get way too hot. It will affect whatever is in the environment negatively.

Converting to a Paleolithic nutritional lifestyle has allowed me to eat a diet that is void of inflammatory foods. Aside from healing "leaky gut" and thus allowing the immune system to calm down, Paleo diets also reduce inflammation in many other ways. I have highlighted a few below,:

Chapter 2 Losing Weight With Paleo

- The diet is high in vitamin D. Vitamin D has been proven to aid in reducing inflammation.

- The diet is high in phytonutrients, many of which have anti-inflammatory effects.

- The immune system reacts with inflammation to factors in the environment that it has been exposed to (pollen, bacteria, molds, etc.). The Paleo diet has the effect of making the immune system less prone to react to these factors and also makes it more effective because it is not over-loaded.

- The Paleo perspective adjusts the Omega-3/Omega-6 proportion to a beneficial ratio and makes it an effective agent in battling inflammatory illnesses. An Omega-3/6 imbalance can result from eating vegetable oils, grain products, and a deficiency of DHA and EPA from animal products.

Yes, I wanted to lose weight and reduce fat by adopting my new lifestyle. I was also looking to get rid of the ailments and issues that had been with me most of my adolescent and adult life. Paleolithic nutrition made this happen for me and it can help you in countless areas of your life and health as well.

Chapter 3 How to Get Started?

I have been asked frequently what step I took when I first started eating under the Paleo guidelines. Getting started, well just *starting* the Paleo program is essentially the most difficult part. Learning about the benefits of Paleo, what and what not to eat, and how it works is a great pre-game strategy; it is not an actual step into this prolific nutritional lifestyle.

Purging all of the non-Paleo foods from our lives seems to be the hardest part, so I recommend diving right in and doing this first. These foods have been so ingrained into our lifestyles and culture, not to mention that some are physically addictive, it is hard to think about living without them. That is why we have to focus on the underlying principle of the Paleo diet: in order to achieve optimum health we need to eat as our ancient ancestors. They lived without any of these foods and so can we.

The unhealthy food that is in your kitchen will get eaten if you leave it there. These foods are quick to prepare and easier to make than healthy Paleo meals. When I am hungry it is much faster to open a box of crackers or make some Ramen noodles than it is to prepare a healthy fresh Paleo meal. Keep your kitchen free of unhealthy foods and packed full of nutrient rich fresh foods. I did this first. By removing all temptations it was easier to make the good stuff and more difficult to consume the bad stuff.

WHAT TO REMOVE

These are not complete lists of course, but will give you a general idea of what to get rid of and what not to forget. Basically throw out everything in a box, wrapper, or bag. Usually if it has more than 3 ingredients or if you cannot pronounce the ingredients it needs to be removed from the premises. When unsure about a certain item, better safe than sorry; just toss it!

Pantry: Chips, pretzels, tortillas, baked goods, peanuts, instant foods, cereal, bread, bagels, pasta, any mixes, canned beans, crackers, granola bars, rice, sugar, anything processed, etc.

Freezer: Ice cream, frozen breakfast foods, pizzas, hot dogs, candy, etc.

Fridge: Processed meats, dairy, juice, all alcoholic beverages, anything sweetened, leftovers, margarine, breads, whole wheat products, condiments, peanut butter, etc.

WHAT TO BUY NOW:

After I got rid of everything in my kitchen that would deter my goal of eating cave-man/woman style I had to replenish my fridge and cupboards with produce and meats that would complement my new lifestyle.

Sticking to the aisles around the perimeter of the store is usually a good idea when shopping at any kind of grocery store. I had never realized it before, but that is where all the fresh produce, fruit and animal protein is located. Also, there are many detailed Paleo food lists that you can print out online. I still keep one in my purse to this day, just in case.

Reading labels is a must-do for any Paleo dieter. For the most part, anything with a label is probably something you do not want to buy. If it does have a label with ingredients that you cannot pronounce, do not purchase it. Here are some things that I keep in mind when I grocery shop:

Chapter 3 How to Get Started?

Best= Zero ingredients

Better= One ingredient

Ok= Two ingredients

Pushing my luck= Three ingredients

No way= Four+ ingredients

Key words to remember when shopping to stock a Paleo kitchen: Organic, grass-fed, pasture-raised, wild-caught, free-range, and raw.

I had to replace everything in my pantry with new ingredients that I would be using in Paleo recipes. I had previewed these new recipes, and if you are anything like me, these ingredients sounded strange. They are staples of the Paleo kitchen and will benefit you in preparing many delicious Paleo meals and snacks. This a list of items that are usually used in Paleo recipes:

-Blanched Almond flour

-Coconut flour

-Almond Meal

-Extra virgin Coconut Oil

-Refined Coconut Oil
-Palm Shortening

-Arrowroot Powder/Tapioca Starch

Chapter 3 How to Get Started?

-Ground Flax meal

-Coconut Milk

-Creamed Coconut

-Unsweetened Coconut Flakes

-Unsweetened Shredded Coconut

-Nuts: Whole Almonds, Pecan Halves, Walnut Halves, Macadamia Nuts, Hazelnuts, Pistachios, Cashews, Brazil Nuts

-Almond Butter

-Raw/Natural Cocoa Powder

-Honey

-Raw Maple Syrup

-Leavening/Spices: Baking Soda, Cream of Tartar, Allspice, Cinnamon, Salt, -Cloves, Cardamom, Ground Ginger, Nutmeg, Vanilla Extract, Vanilla Bean, -Lemon Juice

As for my refrigerator, I stocked it with plenty of grass-feed, free-range, organic meats, wild-caught fish and tons of Paleo-approved fresh produce.

The next thing to consider when I began this lifestyle was that I needed to **start cooking** all of **my own food**. No more convenience foods, no more fast food. I started gathering recipes for quick meals that could be prepared during the week. I started making large meals that would leave lots of leftovers. These leftovers will be your new convenience foods. You can fill your freezer with home cooked meals that can be reheated quickly on busy days.

Now, aside from the kitchen there are two other areas in my lifestyle that needed to be addressed while starting this primal lifestyle: sleep and the dreaded detox.

SLEEP

Getting enough sleep was probably not very difficult for our hunter-gatherer ancestors. For us, it is much more difficult thanks to a toxic diet and the invention of electricity. These two things have left us in a state of sleep deprivation.

Sleep deprivation can cause many problems including: weight gain, hormonal imbalances, heart disease, lowered immune system function, long periods of high cortisone levels, and many more.

If you do not sleep enough, you may have more difficulty in resisting sugary foods that will sabotage your new healthy lifestyle. Also, eating these carb-filled sugary foods will mess up your sleep schedule because they mess with your blood sugar levels. Sleep is a key component of successfully adopting the Paleo lifestyle.

Sleep works together with a nutritious Paleo diet to help the body function at its best. Here are some tips that I used in order to get enough sleep.

1. **I went to bed at the same time every night.**
2. **I made sure my bedroom was super dark, no lights at all.**

3. I made sure that my room had proper air circulation.
4. I cut out all caffeine.
5. I did not drink alcohol.
6. I made sure that I was in bed by 10 p.m. and out of bed by 7a.m.
7. I was up when the sun was up.
8. I stayed away from using any electronics 2 hours before bed and made sure that electronics were not plugged in near my bed.

Getting enough sleep helped me to stay strong when facing temptation at the start of my new ancient eating program. It also helped me to feel more energized throughout the day while my body adjusted to using fat as an energy source.

I found natural therapies to be very helpful in my case as they helped me restore healthy sleep patterns and rejuvenate myself. Getting enough healthy sleep will prevent you from overeating or indulging in unhealthy foods as well (please check out the recommended reading on relaxation with natural therapies at the end of the book).

THE DREADED DETOX

For about 2-3 weeks (maybe longer) when people first start the Paleo diet, most feel tired, frail, and unproductive. I had the same experience. My body was dependent upon sugars and starches for energy. I removed them and my body went into shock. It takes a while for your body to learn how to use fat as an energy source. The body is also releasing toxins during this time; toxins that have been building up for a very long time. Fight urges to give into caffeine and sugar. Stay away from grains. This feeling will not last forever.

After this time period passed I began to notice that something wonderful was happening inside my body. I was feeling energized for most of the day. I was not constantly hungry. I was not craving the sugars and refined carbs, nor was I craving the whole grain foods either. I felt amazing and wondered why I had never done this before. I craved real, whole, energizing, fresh foods. I had done it, and there was no turning back.

The first move to make when implementing the Paleo way of life is simply getting started. When? I say right now. If you do not, today is one more day you could have spent getting your body healthy. It only takes minutes to perform a kitchen overhaul. I went straight to the store afterward and was preparing my first Paleo meal in hours. Why would you delay when the future looks bright?

Chapter 4 Basic Paleo Recipes for Weight Loss and Vitality

I love to cook. Paleo cooking is fun because you can mix and match so many different things to create many different meals. Experimenting with different meat, herb, oil, vegetable combinations is exciting. Of course, everyone loves a good recipe and I will provide some of my favorites.

People who practice Paleo living usually benefit from meal planning. This enables you to have to items you will need for the week. Cooking Paleo meals usually requires mostly fresh ingredients. By planning ahead, you will know everything you will need to get in one trip to the store.

Here are a few tips for Paleo meal planning:

> 1. Make certain to eat a lot of vegetables. Eating Paleo does not mean eat more meat than anything else. Eating vegetables is key.

> 2. Make sure the meat you are eating are lean cuts, not processed meat.

> 3. Pay attention to how *much* fat you are consuming; confirm that you are eating enough of it every day. A clue that you are not getting enough fat is that you are always hungry or never feel full all the way. If this is the case, eat more avocado and coconut.

Chapter 4 Basic Paleo Recipes for Weight Loss and Vitality

4. Try new things. Experimenting with Paleo is fun. Use a meat or vegetable that you have never heard of before. Try a combination that seems unlikely, you may love it.

5. Do not shy away from bacon. Eat plenty of it, it goes with almost everything.

Every day you will be eating breakfast, lunch, dinner and a snack. I appreciate that in Paleo breakfasts can be anything, they don't have to be "breakfast."

Leftovers make a quick breakfast solution. Here a couple of my favorites of each for morning breakfasts, mid-day lunches, and evening dinners. Enjoy!

BREAKFAST

BREAKFAST

#1.Pan-caves

Serves-1

Ingredients:

-1 cup almond flour
-1 egg
-2/3 cup almond milk
-Washed strawberries
-Washed blueberries
-1 banana
-½ cup almond flakes

Instructions:

1. Heat a pan to medium heat. When warm, add almond flakes in order to toast them. When they are toasted, add strawberries and blueberries and heat. Allow the berries to soften up.
2. Put both in a bowl off to the side.
3. Whisk the egg, flour and milk in a bowl until it is smooth. If it appears runny add a spoonful of almond flour.
4. Reheat the pan to a high heat with a bit of oil.
5. Pour batter into the pan, moving it around a bit.
6. It should brown a bit and firm up a tad, then flip.
7. Repeat this step and until you have used all your batter.
8. Top with the toasted almond/berry mixture.

Serve with bacon! Enjoy!

#2. Easy Paleo Scramble

Serves-2,3

Ingredients:

-6 eggs
-1 poblano pepper
-1 onion
-2/3 cup mushrooms
-1/2 cup tomatoes
-2 cups cooked ham

Instructions:

1. Chop pepper, onion, mushrooms, tomato, and ham.
2. Cook the pepper and onion in coconut oil or bacon grease over medium heat until onion is clear.
3. Next put the mushrooms, tomatoes and ham in the same pan and cook until the ham has browned.
4. Lastly, crack the eggs into the pan, scramble with the veggies and tomato until eggs are done. Season to taste.

BREAKFAST

#3.Spinach and Brussels Frittata

Serves-3, 4

Ingredients:

-8 eggs, whisked
-2 cups Brussels sprouts, cut in fourths
-5-6 cups fresh spinach
-3 tablespoons bacon fat
-2 garlic cloves, minced
-1 tsp. garlic powder
-½ teaspoon paprika
-Salt and pepper
-Avocado to garnish

Instructions:

Preheat oven to 375 degrees.

1. Put bacon fat or a few tablespoons coconut oil in a skillet and heat to medium-high. Once heated, add garlic, Brussels sprouts, salt and pepper. Cook until it browns on one side, then flip sprouts to ensure that they brown on all sides (takes approximately five minutes).
2. Add the spinach and put a lid on so that it will steam. Cook for 4 more minutes until the spinach is soft.
3. In a separate bowl whisk eggs, garlic powder, and seasonings. When the vegetables are done, mix them into the egg mixture.
4. Pour the egg/vegetable mixture into a large baking dish or cast iron skillet.
5. Put in preheated oven for 15-18 minutes depending how big the skillet is. Check to make sure it is done by pressing on the middle. If it is done it will push back. Top with avocado. Enjoy!

LUNCH

#4.Spicy Tuna with Artichokes

Serves-2

Ingredients:

-2T Coconut oil
-1/2 red onion (slice as thin as possible)
-Artichoke hearts (however many you like)
-1 Lemon sliced
-2 cloves of garlic sliced
-4 sprigs fresh thyme
-1 ½ lbs. fresh tuna (1 inch cubes)
-1 ½ tsp sea salt
-1 tsp black pepper
-1 tsp cayenne pepper
-3-4 cups steamed veggies

Instructions:

1. Heat 1 Tbsp. of oil and sauté onions for about 3 minutes. Throw in artichoke hearts, lemon, garlic and thyme (cook for about three more minutes). Set aside.
2. Season tuna. Heat the rest of the oil in the same skillet and brown the tuna on all sides, cook to your liking.
3. Add the artichokes, lemon, garlic and thyme to the tuna and mix together. Serve and enjoy!

#5.Guacamole Peppers

Serves-2,3

Ingredients:

-5 small/medium poblano peppers
-2 ripe avocados, cut in half and pits removed
-1/4 cup chopped fresh cilantro
-1/4 cup finely chopped red onion
-1/4 teaspoon salt
-1 cup shredded hearts of romaine

Instructions:

Preheat broiler on High.
1. Put peppers on a broiler pan or cookie sheet. Broil 3 to 4 inches below the heat. Turn a couple of times until the skins blacken and bubble (10 minutes or so). Put in a bowl, cover and let stand (10-15 min). They will be easy to peel now. Leave stems attached.
2. Scoop avocados into a bowl and mash with a fork. Stir in cilantro, onion and salt.
3. Stem and seed one of the peppers and chop. Mix it into the guacamole.
4. Make a slit through one wall of each of the remaining 4 peppers top to bottom and remove seeds. Put romaine in each of the peppers, then fill with a generous 1/3 cup guacamole each.

#6. Mexican Chicken Salad

Serves-4

Ingredients:

CHICKEN
- 1 lb. boneless, skinless chicken breasts
- 1 TBSP oil of your choice
- Salt and pepper

SALSA:
- 1 large tomato, quartered
- 1/2 red onion, cut into large pieces
- 1 jalapeno pepper, stem and seeds removed and halved
- 1 clove of garlic
- 1 small bunch of cilantro leaves
- 1 lime (to squeeze juice from)
- Salt and pepper

Instructions:

Preheat oven to 375.

1. Lightly coat chicken breasts in olive oil and season. Bake in oven 35 to 40 minutes.
2. Chop all salsa ingredients in a food processor, or by hand.
3. Take chicken out of the oven. Once it cools, cut up the chicken and throw into the food processor. Pulse until shredded (or you can also shred chicken with a fork).
4. Mix together chicken and salsa.
5. Refrigerate salad until it is chilled.

Serve over greens of your choice. Enjoy!

DINNER

#7. Zucchini Chicken

Serves-3,4

Ingredients:

-2 T. Coconut oil
-8 drumsticks
-Sea salt and pepper
-1 T. poultry seasoning
-1 yellow onion, cut into big pieces
-4 cloves garlic (chopped or minced)
-1 cup tomatoes (diced)
-5 small zucchini, cut into big pieces

Instructions:

1. Heat coconut oil in a sauce pan. Season drumsticks and then add to pan. Brown on all sides.
2. Sprinkle poultry seasoning over the drumsticks. Add the diced tomatoes, onion, and garlic.
3. Simmer over medium-low heat for 15-20 minutes.
4. Now, add the zucchini. Continue to cook over medium-low heat. Cook for an additional 5 minutes.

Enjoy! I do!

#8. Bacon-topped Meatloaf

Serves-3

Ingredients:

2 lb. Grass Fed ground beef
1 lb. ground pork
2 organic eggs
1 cup almond flour
1 cup tomato sauce
12 slices of bacon (nitrate free)
1 onion, chopped
2x15 oz. roasted tomatoes
1 cup roasted red peppers
5 cloves of garlic
1 tsp cumin
1 tsp oregano

Instructions:

1. Preheat oven to 350 degrees
2. Mix 1 of the 15oz tomatoes, roasted red peppers, garlic, cumin, and oregano in a food processor. Mix the pork, onions, beef, almond flour, eggs and tomatoes in a large bowl.
3. Place into a baking pan (large loaf pan) then salt and pepper.
4. Top with bacon and cook for 45 min.
5. Turn broiler on and place under broiler for 10 min
6. Simmer the rest of the tomatoes in a sauce pan for 15 min.
7. When the meatloaf is done, top with the simmered tomato sauce.
8. Serve with Sautéed Kale (see below)

Enjoy!

#9 Sautéed Kale

Serves-2

Ingredients:

- 2 tablespoons of olive oil or coconut oil
- 1 large onion chopped
- 1 bunch kale cut into 1-inch strips
- ¼ teaspoon sea salt

Instructions:

1. Heat oil over medium heat.
2. Reduce heat to medium low then and add onion.
3. Sauté for 15 minutes until onions have caramelized.
4. Put kale in pan with onions and sauté for 5 minutes uncovered.
5. Cover pot with a lid and cook for 1-2 minutes so that kale is completely wilted.
6. Add salt

Enjoy!

#10. One Dish Fish

Serves- 4

Ingredients:

4 fish fillets (about 1 ½ lbs.) Salmon, Tilapia, Cod (or a mix)
1 cup of cherry tomatoes
2 yellow squash
2 green bell pepper
1/4 cup olive oil
1 Tablespoon apple cider vinegar
1 Tablespoon vodka or gin
Salt and pepper
1 T. tamari soy sauce, coconut aminos, or Bragg's liquid aminos

Instructions:

Preheat oven to 375F.
1. Chop up the fish, squash, and bell pepper into 1 in. cubes.
2. Put all ingredients into a large casserole dish.
3. Bake for 35 minutes uncovered.

Enjoy!

I included very simple, delicious Paleo recipes in order to show that Paleo cooking need not be complicated. I started out with these same recipes. There are many out there to choose from. I sometimes enjoy turning my favorite Neolithic recipes into recipes that fit my Paleo nutritional perspective. I also love coming up with original recipes. It is my hope that the recipes I shared with you will show you that Paleo cooking is fun and easy! Carry on reading to discover more…

Chapter 5 Paleo Healthy Snacks: How to Avoid Cheating?

In a perfect world, snacking in the Paleo lifestyle would be unnecessary. You would be able to always eat the perfect sized meal, packed with the appropriate nutrients that would keep you feeling full until the next one. Well, the world is not perfect and even those who achieve Paleo-perfection sometimes need something to tide them over. Situations like this call for us to have pre-planned snack options to keep us on track.

These snacks are especially important for Paleo-newbies in their first 3-4 weeks to keep them on the right track during moments of weakness. Here are 10 snacks that are easily prepared and some crisis snacks to keep on hand just in case.

1) Roasted Pumpkin Seeds

Full of potassium, fiber and protein, pumpkin seeds are easy to make and delicious. Just heat the oven to 350, coat seeds in coconut oil and spread on a baking sheet for 20 min until they are golden brown. Stir them half way. I add cayenne pepper, but you can add most any spice or seasoning.

2) Tuna and Avocado

They are both super good for you and include protein and healthy fat to keep you full! Just scoop out the avocado into a bowl mix in some tuna and a big squeeze of lemon! I add cayenne and pepper, but season as you will.

3) Kale Chips

My absolute favorite!!! They are super healthy and can help when you want something to munch.

Here is the mini recipe:

-Preheat oven to 350,

-Rip up Kale put in a bowl and drizzle with avocado or coconut oil.

-Bake for twelve minutes. Remove and sprinkle with your favorite seasoning. SO delicious.

4) Good ol' Bacon and Eggs

Use a muffin tray and put 2 bacon strips in each cup then crack and egg inside. Preheat oven to 350 and then bake for 10 min.

5) Veggies and Paleo Hummus

Raw veggies can kill the urge to munch and hummus is never a bad idea (to me)!

Recipe #11

2 medium zucchini, cut up and peeled
½ cup tahini
⅓ cup juice from a lemon
⅓ cup evoo
3 cloves of garlic
2 teaspoons cumin
Salt & pepper (add cayenne if you like it spicy)

Put everything in the food processor, and run until smooth.

EMERGENCY SNACKS

6) Fresh fruit

Always have it washed and ready to eat!

7) Cut vegetables

Will curb a munching craving and are good to have on hand for meals and salads as well. I cut a full bags worth of each on grocery day! Truly a lifesaver.

8) Fresh cold sliced meats

Such a typical Paleo snack idea, but you would be surprised how many people do not think of it. Make sure the brand is Paleo-friendly.

9) Trail mix of nuts and seeds

Mix up your favorites and keep in a container in the pantry. When I know I may be out and about I throw a handful in a snack-sized baggie.

10) A can of tuna

Keep them on hand in the cupboard and in the fridge. Always a winner.

These snacks will keep you from cheating. The options are almost endless but it is always good to have a list to start with and these are my favorites. They will also help you not feel so hungry and fall off of the Paleo wagon easily. The more you see Paleo working for you, the more you will work for it!

Chapter 6 Awesome Paleo Recipes- Back to the Cave!

What was the biggest obstacle in my Paleo dieting adventure? Lack of variety. Yes, I got stuck eating the same stuff all over again, and I would automatically get back to my old unhealthy eating patterns simply because I felt like I was missing something...Then I realized that it takes some time to become Paleo-creative. First, you need guidance- more and more Paleo friendly recipes to keep on track.

This is why I am adding this chapter that will provide you with plenty of super healthy and delicious Paleo recipes for the whole family to enjoy.

Make it easy for yourself and don't make the same mistakes that I was making- there is no point in getting back to where you were before.

It's up to you if you decide to do your Paleo thing full-time or part-time. For example, my wife, Elena is a big fan of the Alkaline Diet. In fact, we have written a bestselling book on how to combine successfully these two eating patterns. (*"Alkaline Paleo Recipes"*)

My suggestion is: prepare your weekly menus on Sundays. Plan your shopping list, food for work, snacks, Paleo treats and dinners that you can have with friends. Invite them over and make them addicted to this amazing diet!

The previous chapter is merely an introduction for beginners. You will find many more paleo recipes here...

Ok ladies and gentlemen, it's time to get back to the CAVE with the following recipes...

Chapter 6 Awesome Paleo Recipes- Back to the Cave!

#12 PALEO YUMMY CAKE

Serves- 5 people, ok, maybe only 3 if they are Paleolithic Athletes...

Ingredients:

-250 Grams of raw almonds

-70 Grams of agave syrup

-The skin of a lemon (you can use 2 lemons as well)

-4 Organic eggs (make sure they are organic, free-range)

-Olive oil (coconut oil is also fine if you are a coconut oil lover!)

-Eco-Dark Chocolate 100% Cacao

Preparation:

1. Preheat oven to 180 º
2. Crush almonds and put aside in a small utensil
3. Whisk the lemon peel, agave and eggs
4. Add crushed almonds and stir
5. Grease the pan with olive oil or some coconut oil (1 tablespoon should do)
6. Pour this paleo batter into the mould and put in the oven, bake for about 15-20 mins.
7. Remove from oven and serve with organic chocolate on top.
8. Enjoy! I always do!

#13 Veggies inna Cave

My wife absolutely loves this dish. I think she was born to be a vegetarian. Now, many people think that Paleo Diet is only about eating meat in exaggerated amounts. I think that it's all about finding balance. So...have no fear when you see a nice plate of fresh vegetables...of course if your salivary glands are looking for meat sensation or you are an athlete, you can add some bacon or tuna as well (optional). However, aside from my Paleo preferences, I am also a firm believer in the Alkaline Diet. Hence I like to detoxify my body and go alkaline from time to time:

Serves- 2,3

Prep time- 15 mins

Ingredients

-1 Onion.

-2 Zucchinis.

-8 Mushrooms.

-4 Asparagus.

-1 Leek.

-Condiments: coarse salt, cumin and olive oil.

Preparation:
1. Wash and chop the vegetables (small medium pieces).
2. Put on the grill (I use the one that does not require using any kind of oil for cooking) using low heat
3. Add salt and cumin. Keep flipping occasionally so that your veggies don't burn themselves to death... (it takes about 10- 15 mins on low heat)
4. Remove when ready and add a drizzle of olive oil on the plate.

Chapter 6 Awesome Paleo Recipes- Back to the Cave!

OPTIONAL: add some bacon or tuna to your veggie mix. You can also use algae (more on algae later)

#14Alkaline Paleo Mix

Here comes another light veggie dish. Again, paleo is not only about eating meat.

Serves- 4

Ingredients:

-1 Piece of broccoli (500 grams).

-4 Medium onions.

-4 Cloves of garlic.

-Curry, sea salt and olive oil.

Prep Time: 20 minutes

Preparation:

1. Put the chopped broccoli, chopped onions and garlic, and a handful of salt in a pan with a pint of water, heat to medium.
2. When everything is slightly "boiling", add some curry, leave for about 2 minutes stirring and turn off.
3. Drain the water into a bowl. /Put aside a few pieces of broccoli for later to garnish the dish when it's ready/.
4. Add a splash of olive oil and a blend the veggies. Add some more salt and oil if needed (taste it first)
5. Serve in bowls, place a piece of broccoli in the center and add a drizzle of olive oil on top.

I also like using coconut oil with this recipe as it gives it really nice, creamy taste!

Irresistible.... It's cool to be healthy, right?

Of course, you can add some bacon or chicken...

#15SALMON ROCKS!

I can never get fed up with salmon. It is a great source of healthy fats and it gives me all the protein I need to for paleo athletic endeavors! My wife also likes it, she is not a big fan of meat, but she absolutely loves fish...

Serves- 2 Paleo athletes

Prep TIME: 15 minutes.

Ingredients

-6 Range eggs.

-6 mushrooms

-6 medium artichokes

-100 Grams of smoked salmon.

-4 Cloves of garlic.

-Salt and olive oil. I also like some rosemary herb.

Preparation:
1. Chop the garlic in small pieces and start frying slightly in a little amount of oil in a flat pan. Keep the heat low.
2. Add the mushrooms (finely chopped) and the artichokes. You may also want to add a pinch of salt.
3. When the juices start coming out of veggies, add salmon (chopped in small pieces)
4. Then add the beaten eggs, stirring with wooden spatula. Do not let them dry completely.
5. Serve with fresh chopped tomatoes and a drizzle of olive oil.

#16Paleo Bacon Brussels Sprouts with Twist

Yes, I admit it, I love bacon! The good thing about Paleo is that you don't have to give it up, quite on the contrary- include it. The reason why bacon is being criticized by many health watchers is that oftentimes it is accompanied by unhealthy processed foods like white bread, butter and crisps (blehh!). These must go of course, as they are off Paleo lifestyle. However, adding bacon to some veggies is a different story. You can satisfy your bacon hunger and keep healthy and slim and the same time. Moreover, this dish is pretty alkaline as well. Not super alkaline of course, but mildly alkaline. To be honest, I think that brussel sprouts are boring this is why I add bacon and make it one of my proffered dishes actually. The total preparation time here is nearly an hour, so I suggest you keep it dish for family and friends dinners and get someone to help you.

Serves-2

Ingredients

-50 gr of bacon, cut into strips or diced in small pieces

-2 shallots or 1 small onion, chopped

-500 gr Brussels sprouts, cleaned and cut in half

-½ to 1 cup chestnuts, roasted and peeled

-fresh thyme (leaves)

-¼ cup chicken broth

-Salt and pepper, to taste

Instructions

1. 1.Preheat oven to 220 degrees.
2. 2.In the meantime, fry the bacon in a frying pan until it's crispy
3. 3.Add the shallots and saute for about 2 minutes, until translucent. Add some broth is necessary

Chapter 6 Awesome Paleo Recipes- Back to the Cave!

4. Increase the heat and add the cabbage, sprouts, chestnuts, thyme and broth, season and stir well with a wooden spoon.
5. Meter skillet (or ovenproof pot that you were using to stir-fry the ingredients) in the oven for about 25 minutes, stirring halfway through cooking spoon, until the sprouts are tender.
6. Serve immediately.

#17Mini Recipe: Guacamole and Bacon

Total Time-10 minutes

Serves- 2,3

Ingredients

-2 ripe avocados

-½ red (or scallions) chopped onion

-A few sprigs of fresh cilantro, finely chopped

-Juice of half a lime

-3 strips of bacon, cooked until they crisp and crumbled

-2 teaspoons spice mixture Merkén, or chili powder or a pinch of ground coriander)

-½ ripe tomato diced (optional / seasonal)

-Salt

Instructions

1. Mix all ingredients, except salt, mashing the avocado with a fork.
2. Try the guacamole and adjust salt to taste, add your spices as well
3. Serve to accompany some sticks of raw vegetables or paleo gluten free crackers.

#18. Creamy Bolognese Sauce

I love Italian food! The good news is that you make paleo-lize it and make it healthy. This recipe traditionally includes cheese, however we will replace it by some almond powder (vegan cheese!). The spices remain the same and so your taste buds will be satisfied!

Total Prep Time

2 hours 25 mins

Serves- 6 people

Ingredients:

-15g (about ½ cup) dried porcini

-1 to 2 stalks celery

-1 medium onion

-3 carrots

-1 red pepper

-4-6 cloves of garlic

-2 tablespoons coconut oil

-2 sprigs of rosemary

-2 bay leaves

-500g minced meat (I used 100% cow pasture, but could be used mixed with beef or pork)

-250ml coconut milk

-1 bottle (700ml) crushed tomatoes

Chapter 6 Awesome Paleo Recipes- Back to the Cave!

-250ml beef stock

-salt

-pepper

-crashed almonds vegan "parmesan" (optional)

Instructions

1. Put the mushrooms in a bowl with boiling water and leave until about 15 minutes to cook, then drain the mushrooms.
2. Cut the remaining vegetables and place in a food processor along with the mushrooms. Grind to a smooth paste.
3. Heat some olive or coconut oil in a pan (medium heat), insert rosemary and bay leaf. Then toss the mushroom paste with vegetables and fry for about 10 minutes. Keep stirring.
4. Increase the heat and add the meat.
5. Add the coconut milk and cook for 5-10 minutes, until thickened. Coconut milk will make it creamy in a paleo way.
6. Then add the crushed tomatoes, broth, salt and pepper. Lower the heat, and let it simmer for about 2 hours, stirring occasionally.
7. Serve with spaghetti of zucchini, squash, roasted sweet potatoes or other vegetables. If you want an occasional cheat, you may sprinkle over some parmesan cheese. If you do paleo full-time, like me, then add some almond vegan cheese.

Enjoy!

Chapter 6 Awesome Paleo Recipes- Back to the Cave!

#19.CLASSIC PALEO Breakfast

There are many varieties of paleo omlettes. This is how I do it...

Serves-2

Ingredients:

-4 eggs (organic, free-range)

-1 tablespoon of organic olive oil

-1 cup of spinach leaves (chopped finely)

-some fresh basil, (chopped)

-1 small avocado

-1 Black pepper

Preparation:
1. Beat eggs in a small bowl.
2. Heat oil in a frying pan (medium heat is recommended) and add the eggs.
3. When the eggs are almost done, put the spinach on one side on top. Add some basil and pepper. Fold in half.
4. Reduce heat and let it simmer for 1 minute.
5. Finally, garnish with some avocado slices.

Enjoy and have a powerful day!

#20. Jamaican Paleolithic Twist

This is a really nice, spicy, tropical paleo friendly meal. Great for dinners with friends!

Serves-4

Ingredients

-4 tablespoons of olive oil (or coconut oil)

-2 cloves garlic, crushed

-2 tablespoons of fresh lemon juice

-1 teaspoon of chili powder

-1 teaspoon cumin

-2 pounds flank steak (striped)

-1 onion, cut into small pieces

-1 red pepper, chopped

-1 yellow pepper, stripped

-1 tomato

-2 tablespoons of dark rum (not really paleo, but..hey..!)

-¼ cup fresh cilantro, chopped

Preparation

1. Place meat in the bottom of a glass dish.
2. 2Mix 2 tablespoons of olive oil with some garlic and lemon juice. Then add some chili powder and cumin and shake the mixture
3. Use it to marinate the meat for about 2 hours (leave in a fridge)
4. Heat 1 tablespoon of your chosen cooking oil (coconut or olive oil) in a skillet Use medium heat

5. Add beef strips and stir-fry.
6. Then add the veggies: onion and peppers(chopped) and keep frying. Stir regularly.
7. Mix tomatoes (peeled and smashed) and rum, I suggest you use a blender or a food processor. Add to your veggies for extra taste and cook for about a minute.
8. Sprinkle with cilantro. Remove from heat and cool down.

Chapter 6 Awesome Paleo Recipes- Back to the Cave!

#21.Cherry Berry Paleo Delight

Craving for sweets? Go for natural, paleo friendly choices...

Serves-4

Ingredients:

-half cup Bing or Rainier cherries, pitted and chopped

-half cup of blueberries

-1 cup golden raspberries

-1 cup of blackberries

-1 teaspoon of sweet almond powder

-½ teaspoon of clove powder

-½ cup of cinnamon

-a handful of mint leaves

-cocoa powder

Preparation:
1. Mix the cherries with berries in a bowl.
2. Add almond powder, clove powder, cinnamon and some fresh mint (chopped) 3. Let cool for about 30 minutes so as to serve it chilled, you can skip that step though
3. Garnish with: cocoa powder or nuts or mint.

Yummy! My kids love it!

Chapter 6 Awesome Paleo Recipes- Back to the Cave!

#24.Shrimp Stuffed Avocados

Attention sea food lovers! You can find something you like in Paleo Lifestyle as seafood plays a crucial role in it. Seafood is a great and healthy source of protein that is low-fat and rich in omega oils. All we need to make sure that our body and mind functions at its optimal levels...

I love this recipe as a healthy snack.
Prep time- 5 mins.

Serves-4

Ingredients:

-4 large, peeled avocados (remove the seed and cut in half)

-2 cups of shrimp (cooked and ready to eat)

-1 tablespoon of fresh lemon juice

-1 tablespoon onion powder

-1 tsp. black pepper

-1 tablespoon paprika

Preparation:
1. Put avocados in a bowl. The internal side should be facing up (remove the seed of course).
2. Mix the shrimp with some lemon juice. Add onions and pepper (chopped).
3. Place shrimp mixture into each avocado, covering it as much as you can
4. Sprinkle the top of each stuffed avocado with paprika before serving.
5. Enjoy!

Chapter 6 Awesome Paleo Recipes- Back to the Cave!

#25.Paleolized Chicken and Vegetable Soup

This is one of my fave dishes for cold winters. It is also a great, natural remedy for colds and flu. I got this recipe from my wife, but of course, I had to add some chicken to make it suitable for carnivorous paleos!

Serves- 6 (or 3 Paleo Athletes, or 3 Paleos Suffering from Flu!)

Ingredients:

-6 cups water (filtered)

-A whole chicken, cut into cubes

-2 cloves garlic, minced

-1 yellow onion, chopped

- 1 bay leaf

-1 tsp. black pepper

-6 fresh tomatoes, diced

- 2 small zucchini, thinly sliced

- 3 carrots, diced

Preparation:

1. Mix some water with the chicken, garlic, onion. Add bay leaf and pepper to spice it up.
2. Bring to boil. Use medium heat
3. Leave it on low about 2 hours, make sure that the chicken is tender
4. Finally, add the remaining ingredients. Simmer for a few minutes
5. Reduce heat

6. 6-Cover and let it simmer for about 10 minutes, or more. Check if the veggies are tender.
7. Serve warm, enjoy!

This section is dedicated to my beautiful wife Elena, who introduced me into Macrobiotic cooking. This section contains delicious Paleo friendly recipes that also take care of your minerals and nutrients intake. You will discover how to **incorporate algae into your Paleolithic Lifestyle.**

Something that I don't really get is when I see people, who think that they are Paleo because they eat large amounts of meat with some occasional veggies. I believe in a balanced diet. Many of my friends gave up on Paleo eventually. When I asked them why, they would normally say that it was boring and "always the same".

I want to show you how much variety you can put into your Paleo-friendly diet.

Algae are great natural source of many macronutrients that our modern, standard diet very often lacks. Even if you think you are healthy as you eat lots of fruits and veggies, there is still something that you can improve.

My experiment with the regular intake of algae was- I felt like 16 again. I am literally bouncing off the walls. Many of my friends suffer from impotence. I always tell them about my nutritional habits and a healthy Paleo lifestyle and how positively it affects my sexual performance. I have never even considered utilizing the blue pill or any kind of pill. I guess that our ancestors did not have to either...

If you are a female and are suffering from PMS, menstrual pain or menopausal issues simply try to include algae into your diet and you will be amazed at the results. Of course I am not saying that algae are the ultimate cure, however they do make sure that our body remains well-nourished.

I made sure that all my recipes taste great so don't get put off by algae!

#26. BEET SOUP AND ALGA DULSE

Ingredients:

-some Dulse seaweed in sheets (about 15 g should be enough)

-1 kg of red beets

-1 cup of coconut milk

-1 clove of garlic

-fresh lemon juice (one lemon)

-white pepper

-herbal salt or seaweed instant

-Chopped chives

Preparation

1. Wash the beets and cook in boiling water so that the skin can be easily removed.
2. Drain and mix it with 1 cup of coconut milk.
3. Blend with the rest of the ingredients and dulse seaweed powder.
4. Add some lemon juice.
5. Optional: I love adding some nuts to this recipe. I have also tried it with some fried bacon (yummy/

#27.AVOCADO SALAD WITH SEA SPAGHETTI ALGA

Salads are easy and quick to prepare and your imagination is the only limit of what can be created...

Serves-4

Ingredients:

-10 g Sea Spaghetti seaweed

-4 avocados

-2 carrots

-a handful of currants

-some olive oil

-lemon

-basil

Preparation:

1. Let the sea spaghetti soak in water for 20 minutes.
2. Peel avocados and cut them into slim sheets. I suggest you spray them with lemon so that they keep their natural color.
3. Wash and peel the carrots. Cut them into sticks.
4. Once the Sea Spaghetti is soaked, drain it and prepare for the salad.
5. Here is how I normally organize the layouts: a few drops of lemon first, followed by Sea Spaghetti, then avocados with carrots, then currants and some olive oil. To garnish-sprinkle it with some fresh basil.

Enjoy!

#28. Apple Paleo Agar Agar Dream Dessert (no sugar or fructose)

Ingredients:

-2 tablespoons agar agar flakes

-150g prunes (pitted)

-6 apples

-juice of half a lemon

-3 tablespoons cream or almond puree or crushed almonds

Preparation:
1. First soaked the sliced plums in filtered water. Next add the agar agar to soak and take some nice flavor.
2. Meanwhile, peel and chop the apples and cook them for about 15 minutes (medium heat). Then process them through a blender adding agar agar and plums (it's easier to achieve a nice, smooth and thin cream when the apples are slightly cooked. I suggest you keep the apple infused water as it is full of minerals and vitamins).
3. Pour this mixture into a mold. Let it cool down.
4. Serve chilled, garnished with small sheets of green apple + a few drops of lemon juice.
5. Add some fresh mint and cinnamon if you like

Enjoy!

#29. Seaweed Salad and Avocado.

This is a super quick and easy prep dish.

Serves-3

Ingredients:

-1 sheet of sea lettuce

-2 avocadoes

-juice of one lemon

-olive oil

-one garlic clove

-4 tomatoes

-2 cucumbers

-4 carrots

Preparation:
1. Soak the lettuce sea alg in filtered water for about 15 mins
2. In the meantime, peel and cut avocados, cucumbers, carrots and garlic in small pieces
3. Drain the soaked alga and mix with the veggies.
4. Sprinkle with some fresh lemon juice and olive oil

Serve immediately

We have a perfect meal for Paleo raw food lovers!

Enjoy!

#30. Kiwi Wakame Paleo Smoothie

Wakame is my favorite alga. I like using it in my smoothies too.

Preparation Time- only 10 minutes

Serves- 2

Ingredients :

- 2 kiwis
- juice of 2 lemons
- 2 banana
- 1 small piece of ginger
- about 6 square cm of wakame (cut it out from wakame sheet)
- coconut milk, half glass
- half glass water
- half teaspoon of chlorella powder (extra energy!)

Instructions:

1. Soak alga wakame in cold water for about 15 mins
2. In the meantime peel and slice the kiwis and bananas and squeeze the lemon juice
3. Blend all the ingredients and don't forget to add some chlorella powder.

Chlorella helped me and my wife quit coffee. If you are a coffee lover, try this recipe in the morning. Your energy will be restored naturally. Lemon juice stimulates the lymphatic system that is a bit sluggish first

Chapter 6 Awesome Paleo Recipes- Back to the Cave!

thing in the morning- hence the feeling of heaviness and tiredness and puffs under the eyes...

Coffee only deplets you of vital minerals. Our ancestors did not need any coffee drugs. Yes, I believe that coffee is a harmful drug. The fact that it is legal, does not mean that it is safe.

Chapter 6 Awesome Paleo Recipes- Back to the Cave!

#31.Japanese Paleo Twist

Another light Paleo option inspired by Japanese Cuisine!

Preparation time- 25 minutes

Serves-2

Ingredients:

-15 g of dried wakame seaweed,

-1 small cucumber

-1 tablespoon of olive oil

-a few drops of lemon juice,

-1-2 teaspoons sesame seeds,

-1 pinch of sugar,

-1 small chilli.

Preparation:

1. Cover the dried wakame seaweed in warm filtered water. Leave to soak between 10 and 20 minutes. Then: drain and rinse in filtered water.
2. Peel the cucumber and cut into thin sticks. Lightly toast sesame seeds. Chop the chilli, avoiding the seeds.
3. Mix the following in a bowl: olive oil sugar and lemon juice. Add the sesame and chili. Mix the seaweed with

This is a really light, refreshing Asian Paleo menu!

#32 Weight Loss Paleo Apple Pudding

Ingredients:

-Fresh, organic apples of your choice (about 1-2 kilos, it's up to you, I like cooking in bulk)

-1 tablespoon of vanilla powder

-Cinnamon (powdered)

-One lemon (we will only need the peel, but you can also use the fruit for some fresh lemon juice to add to this pudding)

-orange juice of 2 oranges

-1 cup of coconut milk

-Agar agar algae in powder. You will need about 2 tablespoons.

Preparation:
1. Wash and peel the apples. Cut them in small pieces and simmer them to make them softer
2. Drain the apples and add the rest of the ingredients, then blend them.
3. Bake in the oven (about 180 degrees) until golden brown.
4. Cool down and put on the fridge
5. Serve cold with some cinnamon or fresh fruits. Enjoy!

Agar-agar is an alga full of nutrients and minerals, it also makes you feel full faster and prevents unhealthy food cravings, this is why I recommend it for weight loss regimes.

Chapter 6 Awesome Paleo Recipes- Back to the Cave!

#33.Paleo Hiziki Time

Ingredients

-½ cup seaweed hiziki, soaked about 20 minutes.

-1 large carrot chopped in fine pieces

-½ cup cooked sweet corn.

-3 Tablespoons of walnuts, peeled and chopped

-A pinch of oregano.

-Olive oil.

-Alfalfa sprouts (one cup)

Preparation:

1. 1.Take the hiziki algae (previously soaked and drained) and boil for about 20 minutes (add 2 cups of water).
2. Add the carrots and olive oil until the water is absorbed.
3. Allow to cool down
4. Add sweet corn, nuts, oregano and alfalfa sprouts.

Chapter 6 Awesome Paleo Recipes- Back to the Cave!

#34.Paleo Seewood Spaghetti

Serves-1,2

Prep time- 30mins

Ingredients:

-10 g. Sea Spaghetti seaweed

-1 zucchini, sliced.

-2 carrots, into strips.

-1 cabbage, finely sliced.

-1 small onion, finely chopped.

-Olive oil.

-Pepper.

-Sal

Preparation:
1. Leave the Sea Spaghetti seaweed to soak for about 20 minutes (use filtered water)
2. Drain the Sea Spaghetti seaweed. Fry in some olive oil, in a pan, (small heat) adding carrots and zucchini.
3. Keep stirring and frying.
4. After a couple of minutes add the cabbage, onion, pepper and salt.
5. I like to add a teaspoon of coconut oil as I like the way it tastes.

Serve immediately!

Chapter 6 Awesome Paleo Recipes- Back to the Cave!

#35. Wakame seaweed salad

Serves- 2 people

Ingredients:

-15 gr. wakame seaweed

-1 cucumber

-1 teaspoon of almond milk

-1 teaspoon coconut oil

-1 teaspoon sesame

-1 small chilli (optional)

Preparation:

1. Let the algae soak in filtered warm water for about 15 mins. Then drain, rinse and put aside.
2. Cut and peel the cucumber into thin pieces. Toast the sesame seeds and mince some chilli if you like spicy.
3. Add the algae and put everything together in a salad bowl.
4. As for the dressing: in a small bowl, mix the coconut oil, sweet almond oil and lemon juice. Add the sesame and chili pepper and minced.

Serve immediately,

Enjoy!

#36. Paleo Sardinas Like whisky!

Prep time: 7 minutes

Serves-2

Ingredients:

-4 sardines

-10 g of dried alga dulse

-1 tablespoon of whiskey

-half a glass of coconut milk

-10 cherry tomatoes (peeled and seeded)

-2 tablespoons of coconut oil

-1 lemon

Preparation:

1. Soak the alga dulse in filtered water for about 15 mins. Then drain, rinse and put aside.
2. Put soaked alga dulse in a blender adding other ingredients. Blend. Add some salt if necessary.
3. Serve the sardines with the sauce and half of lemon to garnish and to sprinkle the dish with fresh lemon juice if necessary.

Enjoy! This is a delicious snack!

#37. Easy Seaweed Salad

Serves-2

Ingredients:

-1 handful of Wakame

-1 handful of alga Hijiki

-1 handful of algae "Atlantic dulse"

-4 baby carrots

- 2 tablespoons of peanuts

-2 tablespoons olive oil

-2 tablespoons orange juice

-salt and pepper.

Preparation:
1. Pour all the algae in a pot filled with warm water and leave to soak for 10 minutes.
2. In the meantime, wash, peel and chop the carrots.
3. Mix all the ingredients in a bowl and add some olive oil, orange juice, salt and pepper.

Chapter 6 Awesome Paleo Recipes- Back to the Cave!

#38. Fishy Paleolithic Taste

Serves-4

Ingredients:

-Fish stock: 750 ml

-Sweet Potatoes: 250 g

-Mild olive oil: 125 ml

-One cucumber

-Various algae (Irish moss, sea lettuce, sea spaghetti ...): 50 g

-Half red and green pepper

-Half red onion

-A handful of chopped chives

-Extra virgin olive oil: 30 ml

Preparation:
1. Wash and peel the potatoes and boil them in the fish stock
2. Once cooked, process them in a blender. Add some mild olive oil to help achieve the desired texture. Set aside. Cool down in a fridge
3. Wash and chop other ingredients and put them in a separate bowl. Add the algae and sprinkle with extra virgin oil.
4. Add the potato creamy cold sauce.
5. Garnish with some chopped chives.

Serve nicely chilled!
Enjoy!

Chapter 6 Awesome Paleo Recipes- Back to the Cave!

#39.Paleo Tuna with Algae

Serves-4

Ingredients:

-4 tuna steaks,

-sesame oil

-1 piece of ginger root the size of a hazelnut,

-extra virgin olive oil

-30 grams of dried sea spaghetti

- 1 red pepper

-2 zucchini

-2 cloves of garlic,

-salt.

-half a cup of coconut oil milk

Preparation:

1. Marinate the tuna with some ginger, pinch of salt, olive oil and garlic. Leave in the fridge for about half an hour.
2. In the meantime prepare the algae: soak them in filtered water for about 20 minutes.
3. Prepare the veggies: cut it in small pieces and stir-fry it on a slow heat together with some garlic. Then add the soaked algae and stir-fry until the saucy consistency is achieved. Blend and add some coconut milk for creamy consistency
4. Serve the tuna with this delicious, creamy sauce that is rich in minerals. Serve warm or chilled.
5. Garnish with ginger paste (I usually blend ginger with some coconut milk)
6. Enjoy! I do!

#40. Sexy Skinny

Serves- 2,3

Ingredients:

-1 small broccoli

-1 small cauliflower

-2 eggs

-olive oil

-1 lemon

-Paprika

Preparation:
1. Boil the broccoli with the cauliflower to make them softer. Use medium heat, a few minutes should do. You don't want them to cook too much
2. In the meantime prepare the paleo mayo: blend one egg with some olive oil and some fresh lemon juice. Then add some paprika.
3. Drain the veggies (you may keep the water for soups and other recipes, it's full of minerals and vitamins!) and put in the baking mold. Cover with our paleo mayonnaise.
4. Bake in the oven (180) until slightly brownish.
5. I like to garnish it with some chopped onions, radish and parsley.
6. This is how my kids felt in love with broccoli..

Serve immediately,

Enjoy!

Chapter 7 Paleo Motivation for Lifetime

Paleo is not just a diet, **it is a lifestyle**. Yet, because it is a different lifestyle than most in our society choose to adopt, it takes **motivation** to continue in it for a lifetime.

Most of my motivation comes from the results I have seen in my own life thanks to Paleo. I have more energy than ever. I have been able to maintain a lean and healthy body. The ailments that plagued me for so long have vanished. This is basically my main motivation. Why wouldn't I want to continue to have all of these things by living a Paleo life?

Write down what you wanted to achieve when starting Paleo. What was the goal? -To be healthy?

- To be lean?

-To be free of disease and allergies?

Update on a semi-regular basis. Evaluate on a regular basis whether or not you have gained or achieved your goal and keep the focus on how happy you are with your new life. Always read it when you feel your resolve fading.

Keep your Paleo diet interesting. This helped me immensely. Use different methods to cook your meats and vegetables: grilling, braising, sautéing, stir-frying, roasting, slow cooking, steaming, broiling and poaching are all awesome ways to keep variety in your meals in order to stay motivated.

Mimic techniques that restaurants use to create an eating experience as opposed to just a meal. It helps me to enjoy my food rather than just having something to eat. Here are some ways to create your own eating experience:

-Use garnish! You can make a beautiful presentation on your plate in your own kitchen.

-Turn a boring serving of food into a beautiful meal that you can enjoy. Instead of throwing salad into a bowl, put it on the plate.

-Use multi-colored salad ingredients and arrange them on a plate with a decorative drizzle of dressing.

-Or, instead of piling vegetables next to a piece of meat, make an arrangement around the meat or on top. An edible art piece!

-Garnishes can be part of the meal. Use roasted nuts, citrus fruits sliced in swirls, or fresh herbs.

-Use a beautiful table setting to make your meal inviting.

-Pick out some cheap, pretty prints or colors.

-Visit a thrift store and find some vintage plates, serving bowls, or glasses to make an everyday dinner feel special.

-Put a pitcher of water on your table to bring the restaurant-feel home.

-Add lemon, lime, mint, or cucumber to your water glasses. It makes your beverage healthier and more inviting.

Eating in courses is not just for eating out or a holiday meal. Try it every day. Take time to enjoy and appetizer or a salad before bringing out the main dish. Take a few minutes between courses as you would dining out. The longer you take to enjoy your food, the easier it is for your brain to recognize that it is full. You will eat less while enjoying yourself more.

Chapter 7 Paleo Motivation for Lifetime

These tips are only a few of the ways you can keep yourself motivated as you continue in your healthy Paleo lifestyle. My main motivation is found in my results. The beautiful part of result-based motivation is that it is right there with me all of the time.

The Paleo Diet can be also successfully combined with The Alkaline Diet.

We have a free PDF eBook for you to enjoy that will teach you how to create alkaline-paleo balance for optimal health:

www.holisticwellnessbooks.com/bonus

Bonus Chapter: NLP for Weight Loss

NLP Techniques For Successful Weight Loss?

I hope that this chapter will provide you with some additional weight loss motivation tools that come from Neuro-Linguistic Programming(NLP). There is no theory here, only some practical examples for you to start applying.

Thanks to a **boosted motivation level**, I was on my way to the "new me." At the beginning of the process I realized that every day I felt as if I was battling my old eating habits. I would over eat. Consuming more calories than I was burning was stifling my goal. Eating the wrong foods was also keeping me from achieving physical wellbeing. I used a specific technique to change my bad eating habits. It is referred to as the Swish Pattern.

The **Swish Pattern** is a useful tool in changing old bad habits easily. It is a technique where you replace an undesirable habit for one you would prefer to have. I wanted to replace my unhealthy eating habits (junk food and over-eating) with healthy eating habits (energy foods and eating healthy portions). This tool helped me to change my thoughts and thought process regarding these habits, which in turn changed the bad behavior.

Bonus Chapter: NLP for Weight Loss

SWISH PATTERN

First, choose the habit/behavior that you desire to replace. Visualize it in your mind. Be in the moment of acting out this behavior. Use your five senses to recognize exactly what it feels like. What emotions do you have? Isolate a certain, vividly detailed image of yourself in the midst of engaging in this habit. For me, it was imagining myself shoving pizza into my mouth. Make sure you recognize that this is something you have done in the past and that you want to keep it there. Take a mental picture.

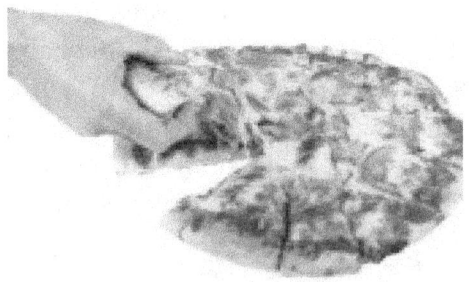

Next, using all of your senses again, create another image of yourself being successful by replacing that bad eating habit with a healthy one. This will be your replacement snap shot. It is vivid, intense, and vibrant. In mine, I had eaten well and used proper portions. I was healthy and energized thanks to making good choices in regard to food. I stepped outside of this picture to see myself in it. At the bottom corner of the new image, you will place a tiny version of yourself in the midst of your bad habit. This tiny picture is dark and colorless.

A Healthy and Balanced Meal or...

Indulging in Unhealthy Habits...?

Now, re-visualize the first picture, the old you. At the bottom corner, darken the future picture (of you and your replacement behavior) and make it small. You can still see it but it is darker. Put yourself back into the poor emotional state that you are currently in. This is currently the big image. You should be feeling all of the self-defeating emotions associated with your bad habit like disappointment and self-loathing. Fully connect yourself with that moment.

Now, instantaneously switch the two images. Bring back the "new you," with your replacement behavior. Make it huge and colorful, full of everything to stimulate your senses. Shrink the picture of your unwanted behavior at the same time, moving it back into the corner and darken it. When you do this, make a "swwwwwissssssssshhhhhhhhh" sound. As I did this I would mentally jump into the replacement behavior image. The picture of you in the future is now the present. The old behavior is in the past, exactly where you want it to be.

I repeated this several times. Switching the pictures and jumping into my new behavioral image while "swooshing." Gradually increase the speed of the switch. Each time I was doing it faster and faster. Eventually it will become instantaneous. Replacing your bad eating habit will be as simple as that.

SETTING AN ANCHOR

Another Neuro-linguistic Programming technique I used on a consistent basis during my weight loss journey was Anchoring. Setting an anchor was immensely beneficial to me and I hope that it is for you as well. It helped me to get back the feeling of being motivated, healthy and happy like I used to be when I was in shape and healthy years ago. This technique helped to keep me driven during my weight loss program. The beauty of this process is that if one anchor does not produce the results you are looking for, it can always be replaced.

Anchoring Facts:

- They can be produced artificially or naturally (due to events).

- They can occur because of a single emotionally charged event or subconsciously through repetition, for example: advertising.

- Needs to be repeated; it can fade with time.

- Make sure you set the anchor when the feeling you want to reinforce is at its peak.

- Choose a very intense memory.

- Make sure that the stimulus you are using is as exclusive as possible. Don't use something you do all of the time.

- I stacked (set) my anchors for approximately 30 minutes; the longer the duration of repetition the better.

1. Choosing a memory- I remembered a time I was at the gym and was asked to be a trainer because I was at my physical best. You choose your own. Make sure it was emotionally intense.

2. Reliving the memory- Associate yourself with the memory. Be in that moment and see it through your own eyes. This made my feelings more intense. I made the picture of the event extremely colorful, large and bright. I intensified my feelings to the maximum.

3. Anchoring the memory- When I felt my emotions at their peak, I pinched the back of my hand. That was my trigger. You can do whatever works best for you: rub your earlobe, grab your knee, etc.

4. Stop at your peak- Release your trigger when your emotion peaks. I had to practice this step a few times before I had it down.

5. Testing the trigger/anchor- I stopped for a while and thought about something else, then used my trigger. If anchoring was successful, it will bring you directly back to that lovely emotional state immediately.

6. Repeat. - Repeat this several times. To make my anchor stronger and more powerful, I set 3-4 memories of times when I felt the same way to that identical trigger.

Anchoring was the most effective way to put myself in a motivated, positive mind set during my weight loss program. I used it almost every day, throughout the day. My trigger helped me be able to feel awesome and driven on demand. What better way to make it through a weight loss program?

SELF-CHECK

An additional way I used NLP ideas in my weight loss program was to check in with myself every day. I needed to make sure that I was staying on track. I would think about and ask myself these key questions:

1. What do I desire?
2. How will getting that help me?
3. What obstacles are keeping me from getting it?
4. What is essential to me?
5. What is working best in this situation?
6. What could be enhanced?
7. What resources am I going to utilize?

Self-evaluation is necessary to achieve any goal. Success in the short or long term requires that questions be asked and answers be evaluated. Then, if necessary, redirection must occur.

If you liked this chapter, then you will also like my book dedicated to Neuro-Linguistic Programming:
http://amzn.to/JURuPi

Bonus Chapter: NLP for Weight Loss

Don't forget to pick up your FREE GIFT...

Free Complimentary eBook

Download link:

www.holisticwellnessbooks.com/bonus

Problems with your download?

Contact us: elenajamesbooks@gmail.com

Conclusion

Thank you again for downloading and reading this book!

I hope this book was able to help you to give you a solid beginning in understanding what the Paleo lifestyle is all about. It is not just a diet. It is a perspective on life and how to live it to the fullest. Paleo is not just the newest fad diet, it is the oldest, healthiest way to eat!

It is my desire that the recipes and tips included sparked something inside of you. **This is only the tip of the iceberg!** The more you learn, the more you will want to put it into practice.

I encourage you to jump right in and get started. You have nothing to lose but weight and health problems, and everything to gain; health, wellness and vitality for the rest of your life!

We were biologically designed to process certain foods in order to maintain maximum health. I hope you have realized, as I did, that it is not a matter of failing at previous diets; "diets" themselves are failures by design. The only way to achieve success is to model what was successful. For us as human beings, it is to eat as our ancient Paleolithic ancestors; free of disease, depression, allergies, and obesity.

I did it. I am doing it. You can too!

Thank you and good luck!

James Adler

Follow us at:

www.YourWellnessBooks.com

www.ingramcontent.com/pod-product-compliance
Lightning Source LLC
Chambersburg PA
CBHW071453080526
44587CB00014B/2090